A
SEASONED
CHEF

A
SEASONED
CHEF

Recipes and Remembrances
from the Chef and Former Co-owner
of New York's Famous
Le Cirque Restaurant

JEAN VERGNES

DONALD I. FINE, INC.
NEW YORK

PERMISSIONS

Page xviii: Ken Feil, The Washington *Post*.
Page 5: Ken Feil, The Washington *Post*.
Page 76: Courtesy *Vogue*. Copyright © 1961 by The Condé Nast Publications, Inc.
Page 84: Reprinted from *Mirror Magazine*. Copyright © 1954 by King Features
      Syndicate, Inc.
Page 87: Bill Mark.
Page 89: Jean Lacombe.
Page 152: Mark Kauffman, *Life*. Copyright © 1965, Time, Inc.
Page 157: Hans Namuth.

Library of Congress Catalogue Card Number 87-46025
ISBN: 1-55611-061-8

Manufactured in the United States of America

10 9 8 7 6 5 4 3 2 1

This book is printed on acid-free paper. The paper in this book meets the guidelines for permanence
and durability of the Committee on Production Guidelines for Book Longevity of the Council on
Library Resources

Design by Stanley S. Drate/Folio Graphics Co., Inc.

*To my wife, Pauline, and
my sons, Robert and Roger,
who put up with a chef's
hours all these years.*

ACKNOWLEDGMENTS

I am indebted to many people in the making of this book. Most especially, my son Roger, his wife Sharon, and Andrew Hoffer, who spent many an hour helping me convey my story. I would also like to express my gratitude to my publisher, Donald Fine, and my editor, Rick Horgan, both of whom recognized that my story was worth telling and gave me the opportunity to tell it.

PERSONAL HISTORY

Jean Ulysse Vergnes
Born November 29, 1921
Rives, Isère, (Dauphine) France

Came to U.S.A. October 1950.
Became an American citizen in 1955.

PLACES OF EMPLOYMENT	POSITION HELD
Grenoble, France	2 Years Apprenticeship
Hotel Raphael (Paris, France)	1st Commis Saucier
Rest. La Cigogne (Paris, France)	Saucier
Rest. La Cabaret (Paris, France)	Garde-Manger
Rest. Le Perigord (Paris, France)	Poissonnier
Rest. Lareine Pedauque (Paris, France)	Saucier
Hotel Du Golf (Deauville, France)	Rôtisseur
Hotel Royal (Evian Le-Bains, France)	Saucier
Hotel Majestic (Chamonix, France)	Saucier
Rest. La Belle Terrace (Denmark)	Saucier
Castle Harbor Hotel (Bermuda)	Chef Tournant
Waldorf-Astoria (New York City)	Saucier
Gogi's La Rue (New York City)	Rôtisseur
La Vie En Rose (New York City)	Assistant Chef
The Colony Restaurant (New York City)	Executive Chef
Stop & Shop, Inc. (Boston)	Executive Chef
Irving Trust Co. (New York City)	Food Services Center Manager
Maxwell's Plum (New York City)	Executive Chef
Le Cirque Restaurant (New York City)	Executive Chef/Owner
Famiglia Industries (New Jersey)	Vice President–Product Development

AWARDS

Le Grand Prix de France 1958
Le Grand Prix de l'America................................ 1959
Commanderie des Cordons-Bleus 1964
Member de L'Académie Culinaire de France.................. 1970
Member de L'Association des Maîtres Cuisiniers de France 1973
Mérite Agricole 1977
Chef of the Year... 1978

Association des Maîtres-Cuisiniers de France
8, Rue de Rome, 8 — PARIS (8ᵉ)

BREVET DE MAITRISE

Vu les articles 5, 6, 7 et 12 des Statuts, et 1 à 5 du Règlement Intérieur,
Vu la délibération de la Commission spéciale en date du 19 Juin 1973

Monsieur *Jean-Ulysse Vergnes*
né le 29 novembre 1921 à Rives (Isère)
est reconnu Maître-Cuisinier.

Paris, le 15 Décembre 1973

Par le Président,
Le Secrétaire Général :

Le Président

Association des Maîtres-Cuisiniers de France
8, Rue de Rome, 8 — PARIS (8ᵉ)

Le Président du Comité Exécutif, président de l'Association,
Vu les articles 5, 6, 7, 11 et 12 des Statuts,
Vu le Règlement Intérieur,
Sur la proposition de la Délégation Générale de l'Association aux Etats-Unis en date du 18 octobre 1977
Vu la délibération du Comité Exécutif en date du 10 Janvier 1978
Décide de reconnaître,

Monsieur *Jean Vergnes*
né le 29 novembre 1921 à Rives (Isère)
Chef de l'année

Paris, le 12 Janvier 1978

Le Président

Le Délégué Général
aux Etats-Unis

Par le Président,
Le Secrétaire Général

RÉPUBLIQUE FRANÇAISE

ORDRE DU MÉRITE AGRICOLE

LE MINISTRE DE L'AGRICULTURE,

par arrêté en date du *28 Janvier 1972*

a nommé Monsieur *Vergnes Jean Ulysse*

Chevalier de l'Ordre du Mérite Agricole.

Paris, le *7 Février 1972*

Le Secrétaire du Conseil de l'Ordre

G. ANDRÉ

LE MINISTRE DE L'AGRICULTURE

ACADÉMIE CULINAIRE DE FRANCE
DIPLOME

Décerné à Monsieur *Vergnes Jean*

le haut Conseil Culinaire

CONTENTS

FOREWORD

Jean Vergnes is a longtime professional colleague and one of my closest friends.

We became *chefs de cuisine* at the same time—he at the renowned Colony Restaurant, which was owned by Gene Cavallero; I at Henri Soulé's famed Le Pavillon. Both restaurants were considered among the best in the country at the time, and they served as the training grounds for an entire generation of American and French chefs.

Jean and I are more than just friends and colleagues; indeed, we are soulmates, for we share a culinary philosophy rooted in the time-honored French apprenticeship system. In our day young cooks—the lofty term *chef* was not something bandied about loosely—started when they were knee-high to a stock pot. I left my native Burgundy at age fourteen to apprentice at the Paris restaurant called Drouant. Jean had a similar experience at an equally tender age. The rigidly defined system of classic French cooking that we inherited has served us well. Young cooks today with culinary school diplomas may view it as somewhat anachronistic, but classic French cuisine is without question the mortar upon which all of today's cooking is based—in the same way Latin is the foundation for the ever-evolving Romance languages.

Jean's culinary capacity is vast. We have cooked together many times both in my home and in Craig Claiborne's kitchen, and many of his recipes have found their way into the food pages of the New York *Times* and in cookbooks of Times Books. While his roots are in the classics, Jean has shifted gears gracefully over the years to keep up with trends. He has embraced the modern style of light and herbaceous cooking with grace and aplomb, always being contemporary—but never faddish. That, to my mind, is the mark of a great chef.

Jean collaborated with Sirio Maccioni in the opening of Le Cirque, one of the great restaurants of New York. One of my fondest memories is of our hunting trip to Nova Scotia some ten years ago when, along with Sirio, Craig Clairborne and Fulvio Nanni, I had the privilege of seeing Jean reproduce his famous recipe for Pasta Primavera.

This book, lovingly written with Jean's son, Roger, recounts these and other stories from those heady days in post–World War II New York and presents wonderful, accessible recipes either conceived of or refined by Jean. It is also a valuable history of the rise of French cuisine in America, of which Jean, my valued friend, was so much a part.

                                        —PIERRE FRANEY
                                        East Hampton, New York
                                        July 18, 1987

To get into best society,
one has either to feed people,
amuse people, or shock people.
—Oscar Wilde

I

THE OPENING OF LE CIRQUE RESTAURANT

I will always remember the night of March 20, 1974, with great fondness. There was an air of excitement and tension in the kitchen as we began the *mise en place* for the opening meal. Some of the deliveries were late, and as happens with any new kitchen and crew, there were kinks in the preparation. The tension could be felt in the dining room as well, where my partner, Sirio Maccioni, gave last-minute instructions to the carpenters working on the banquettes. As I looked around at the work left to be completed, I worried that the preparations wouldn't be finished in time.

The guests were scheduled to arrive for cocktails in half an hour. The dining room was in such disarray that when Craig Claiborne arrived several minutes early he said to me, "Jean, are you sure you're opening tonight?" We laughed; it was indeed a circus within Le Cirque.

Among the guests Sirio and I had invited were fifty prominent members of New York's select group of wine connoisseurs, the Confrerie des Chevaliers du Taste Vin. The group included such notables as Clifford Weihman, Edward Benenson, Richard de Rochemont and David Peck. Also invited were New York real-estate magnate William Zeckendorf Jr., himself a member of the Chevaliers

1

du Taste Vin, and his wife. William was the owner of the newly renovated Mayfair House apartment/hotel of which Le Cirque was a part. He had played a key role in bringing Sirio and me together and in constructing the 95-seat facility, with its separate entrance on Sixty-fifth Street, that was to be Le Cirque.

Several members of the gastronomic profession would be in attendance as well, among them Craig Claiborne and Pierre Franey of the New York *Times*, Robert Misch, Professor Thomas Ahrens and Gordon Bass. Many of these guests had been patrons of the Colony Restaurant, where Sirio and I had been employed during the 1950s and '60s. Sirio and I knew that if we could regularly attract this elite clientele—the same clientele that had been displaced by the closing of *grand luxe* restaurants like The Colony, Le Pavillon and the Café Chauveron—Le Cirque would be established as a respected, upper-scale restaurant.

For the opening-night dinner, I chose dishes that were not overly difficult to prepare. No false haute cuisine was attempted. Rather, the emphasis was placed on simplicity and quality. I chose a delicate lentil soup as an appetizer, followed by striped bass au beurre blanc, entrecôte sautéed with green pepper corns, and a variety of cheeses. Dessert consisted of hot ginger soufflés. By all reports, the dinner, which was complemented by Burgundies and Sauternes, was enjoyed by everyone.

Despite the glitches that mar any restaurant's debut, our opening was judged a success. Within weeks we were attracting the biggest names, the wealthiest people and the most fashionable groups. The roster of luminaries included the late Duchess of Windsor, the late Princess Grace of Monaco, Lady Keith, Countess Crespi, Colonel (former Prince) Serge Obolensky, David Rockefeller, Salvador Dali, President Nixon, Frank Sinatra, Elizabeth Taylor, Gregory Peck, the Vanderbilts, Astors, Fords, Bloomingdales, Rockefellers and Kennedys, to name a few. Anybody who was somebody wanted a table at Le Cirque. We were booked solid for lunch and dinner six weeks in advance. Sirio and I were astounded at how quickly Le Cirque was becoming the next "meeting place" of the prominent.

There were those, in the beginning, who were skeptical of our chances of surviving. Indeed, reading about all the restaurants that closed that year was much like reading a daily obituary column. The question that continually presented itself was: Can an upper-scale restaurant with a large overhead still succeed? As Le Cirque proved, the answer was yes.

Undoubtedly a large factor contributing to our success was the rave reviews we received early on from such notables as Craig Claiborne, Gael Greene, Jay Jacobs, William Rice and Malcolm Forbes, who wrote in his magazine:

> *New Yorkers—this great addition [Le Cirque] to the New York posh restaurant plateau is making it, despite the heavy odds these days of being heavily overheaded. A great oasis for the midtowners who need to talk business, here you can hear each other in a good, gracious place.*

David Breul, editor of *Avenue* magazine, noted:

> *Le Cirque is not at all what it sounds like. The name means "the circus," and this little restaurant could hardly be called that. It's too elegant, too chic . . . While others boast of a rooftop view or their crystal chandeliers, Le Cirque shuns the razzle-dazzle approach. Yet there's plenty of fine cuisine . . . one gets the feeling that it's a gold mine.*

Stendhal, writing in his column in the *Daily News*, said:

> *There is something wonderful about Le Cirque that goes beyond wine and food. The men who operate the establishment love the place, and they are genuinely fond of pleasing their customers . . . While Le Cirque is frequented by society's elite . . . the most obscure corner table will get the same devoted attention and same smooth professional service. When Sirio and Jean say they hope you will return again soon, they mean it.*

And gossip columnist Jack O'Brian added:

> *In a recession era wherein scads of famed restaurants have failed, it's heartening to see a brace of ambitious lads open a distinctively fine gourmet restaurant and succeed right off.*

Such strong critical support helped to strengthen our position in the volatile restaurant market.

People often ask me why I think Le Cirque became such a phenomenon so quickly. I find it hard to point to just one thing. My feeling is that our success was attributable to several factors. I believe one key reason behind our success was the background that Sirio and I had. Sirio and I were experienced professionals who took great pride in our craft. As I've said, we had both worked at the famed Colony restaurant, Sirio as maître d' and I as executive chef. Many of the people we were attracting to Le Cirque had also been clients of The Colony. We referred to them fondly as "the old brigade." When The Colony closed, these people lost their favorite place to dine and socialize. I think that Le Cirque provided them with a new meeting place, one that featured the same ambience and luxury that The Colony had been so famous for. Of course, these people were already familiar with, and trusting of, Sirio's and my abilities, so Le Cirque was something of a natural choice.

To please former patrons of The Colony whom we knew would make up a portion of Le Cirque's clientele, I served some of my old recipes, such as Seafood Crepes, Chicken Gismonda, Tripes à la mode de Caen and others. Sirio and I were sure they'd ask for them. Yet it was not our intent to make Le Cirque a clone of The Colony. In Le Cirque we tried to create something that reflected our personalities. We did not set out to make it *the* place. We merely wanted to make it a good place.

Another reason, I think, for Le Cirque's huge success was the decor of the dining room, designed by the renowned Ellen Lehman McCloskey. With the name Le Cirque in mind, Ellen chose to duplicate the beige and peach monkey murals of the Singerie Room of the Palace of Versailles. The elegant and sedate decor, with its feminine appeal, instantly attracted attention.

But to say that the success of Le Cirque is due to this reason or that reason ignores the larger picture. There was a certain energy level that one experienced when entering Le Cirque's dining room. Every person on our reservation list was a VIP. In a single night I would say good evening to the Duchess of Windsor at one table and David Rockefeller at another; I would suggest a night's special to Jackie Onassis at yet another, and on and on, night after night.

Sirio and I greet regular Le Cirque clients, Margaret Truman Daniel (front) and Gurie Lie Zeckendorf.

There was an ever-present partylike atmosphere, with the electrifying air of money, glamor and fame radiating in and around the closely spaced tables and banquettes.

Le Cirque had its own unique fetelike personality that separated it from all the other elegant French restaurants in New York, making it the phenomenon it still is today. For me as a chef, to have become an owner of a restaurant that attained such heights as Le Cirque did from its outset was a dream come true.

OPENING NIGHT MENU

Lentil Soup

◆

Bar Rayé Poché Beurre Blanc

◆

Entrecôte with Green Peppercorns

◆

Soufflé au Gingembre

Lentil Soup

1 tablespoon butter
1 medium onion, coarsely chopped
1 carrot, finely chopped
½ leek, diced
1 small bay leaf
   Pinch of thyme
2½ quarts beef or chicken broth
1 lb. lentils, washed and picked over
4–5 pork bones; with some meat attached
   Salt and freshly ground pepper to taste

1. Melt the butter in a soup pot and then add the onion, carrot, leeks, bay leaf and thyme. Let the vegetables simmer until softened, about 5 minutes.

2. Add the broth, lentils, pork bones, salt and pepper, and cook gently for about 45 minutes to 1 hour. When the lentils are soft remove the pot from the stove.

3. Remove the bones from the broth and cut the meat off into bite sizes. Return the meat to the soup.

4. Return the pot back to the stove and simmer soup for another 5 minutes.

SERVES 8 TO 10

Bar Rayé Poché Beurre Blanc
POACHED STRIPED BASS WITH WHITE BUTTER SAUCE

1 small onion, sliced
⅓ cup sliced carrots
⅓ cup chopped celery
½ cup coarsley chopped leeks
½ cup dry white wine
¼ cup vinegar
¼ cup parsley sprigs
6 crushed peppercorns
   Salt to taste
   Water to cover fish
4 lb. striped bass, cleaned and scaled

1. In a large skillet, add the vegetables, wine, vinegar, seasoning, and half of the parsley, to the water. Simmer for 10 to 15 minutes.

2. Wrap the striped bass in cheesecloth and place in the boiling liquid. Lower the heat, cover, and simmer gently for about 10 to 20 minutes.

3. Remove the skillet from the heat and put aside for about 10 minutes.

4. Remove the striped bass carefully—unwrap and dress on a fish platter. Decorate with the remaining ⅛ cup of parsley.

SERVES 4

NOTE: This recipe can be served with Beurre Blanc (see page 33) or Lobster Sauce (see page 222).

Entrecôte with Green Peppercorns

2 sirloin steaks (10 to 12 oz. each)
Salt to taste
2 tablespoons butter
1 teaspoon finely chopped shallots
1½ tablespoons green peppercorns
1 tablespoon cognac
¾ cup heavy cream
2 tablespoons Brown Sauce (see page 66)

1. Sprinkle salt on both sides of the steak.

2. Heat 1 tablespoon of butter in a large, heavy skillet. When the butter is hot, sauté the steaks for 2 to 3 minutes on each side until medium rare.

3. Remove steaks from the skillet and put on a platter in a 180° F oven.

4. Add the shallots to the skillet and simmer for 1 minute, add the cognac and light it on fire. When the flames go out, add the green peppercorns and cream, and bring to a boil. Reduce the sauce for 1 minute and then add the Brown Sauce, and let that reduce to the consistency of syrup.

5. Lastly, add the remaining butter and blend gently into the sauce. Pour over the steaks.

SERVES 2

Soufflé au Gingembre
GINGER SOUFFLÉ

10 tablespoons butter
1 cup flour
2¼ cups milk
1 tablespoon grated fresh ginger or 1 teaspoon
  ground ginger
8 eggs, separated
4 tablespoons chopped candied ginger
1 cup sugar

1. Preheat oven to 375° F.

2. Rub the bottom and sides of a 10-cup soufflé dish with 1 tablespoon butter. Place the dish in the refrigerator and let chill.

3. Add the remaining butter to a mixing bowl and add the flour. Work the mixture with the fingers until smooth and thoroughly blended. This is called a beurre manié. Set aside.

4. Pour the milk into a saucepan and add the ginger. Stir and bring to a boil. Add the beurre manié gradually to the milk mixture, about 1 tablespoon at a time, stirring rapidly and constantly with a wire whisk. Continue until all the beurre manié is added and the sauce is quite thick and smooth. Cook, stirring often, about 5 minutes. Remove from the heat and add the yolks, stirring rapidly with the whisk. Return to the heat and cook, stirring, just until the sauce return to the boil.

5. Spoon the sauce into a mixing bowl. Fold in the candied ginger.

6. Beat the whites until stiff and gradually add ¾ cup of sugar, beating constantly. Add about half the whites to the sauce, stirring and blending well. Fold in the remaining whites.

7. Remove the soufflé dish from the refrigerator. Add remaining ¼ cup sugar and swirl the dish this way and that to coat the bottom and sides. Shake out excess sugar.

8. Spoon and scrape the soufflé mixture into the prepared dish. The mixture will more than fill the dish. That is all right. Smooth it over.

9. Place soufflé in the oven and bake 20 minutes. Reduce the heat to 350° F; continue baking 10 to 15 minutes longer. When served, the soufflé will be quite moist in the center. For a firmer soufflé, continue baking another 10 minutes or longer.

SERVES 6 TO 10

As a young apprentice at the Restaurant Phillipe in Grenoble.

II

APPRENTICESHIP

My dream of someday becoming a chef and restaurant owner took many years, and a great deal of work, to be realized. My early years followed a pattern common to many of my confreres: parents in poor circumstances, apprenticeship at the age of thirteen and a ten- to twelve-hour workday, seven days a week, without pay. However, I never look back on that time with bitterness, but rather with profound affection. My apprenticeship instilled in me a strong sense of discipline, love for my craft and a knowledge of the French culinary tradition that could not have been learned properly any other way.

I was born on a farm in a little town named Rives, which is just outside of Grenoble. My father, who worked as a railroad trackman, also raised chickens, rabbits, ducks and other poultry and game. Though we were quite poor—my parents never owned their house—we were quite content. My father kept his own garden and, like many of the French country people, we obtained much of what we ate from our garden and the livestock we raised. Very early in my youth my father ingrained in me a strong work ethic. There were many farm chores to be done and little or no time to play with friends.

It was my mother who did all the cooking. I've never known anybody who could cook better than she. Since we had so little of anything else, the ritual of preparing and eating meals was something almost sacred. I remember my father telling my brothers, Roger and Lucien, and me that dinner would be at six o'clock. If we were one minute late we would not eat that evening. Though I tried always to be on time for each meal, there were nights that I went to bed hungry. But the meals I was fortunate to be on time for remain fixed in my memory. One dish my mother often made was *gateau de foie*, a chicken liver loaf with shallots, parsley, sorrel and spinach, served with a light tomato sauce. I also remember—with mouthwatering fondness—her veal kidneys, pâtés, terrines, head cheese, blood sausage and andouillettes. *Je ne pourrais manger que ça*—I could eat nothing but that.

Even now the image of my father seated at the dinner table, sipping a glass of wine, remains vivid. This was an image that reflected his way of life. He would always use the same glass. Nobody else was allowed to use it. When he was done with it he would simply rinse it with water and let it dry on the shelf. In the morning he would once again take the same glass, and as my brothers and I cleaned our teeth, he would pour some schnapps into it, gargle a bit and then swallow. He did this every morning. I often asked him, "Why can't I do like you do?" *"En bon temp,"* he would reply. In good time.

I remember at about age nine or ten making my first attempts at cooking. My brother Roger and I tried—not very successfully at first—to make pastry tarts. By the time I was twelve I was preparing Hollandaise sauce, roasting meats and cooking vegetables at my aunt and uncle's bistro in Grenoble. I recall my uncle often telling my parents, "Put your boys in the kitchen; they'll be sure they're going to eat." It was the opportunity of working in their bistro that instilled in me the desire to learn more about the culinary trade. But I confess, I also longed to go to Grenoble to see all the people. The city provided so much more in the way of excitement and things to do than the small town in which I was brought up. I was determined to make something of my life, and I realized that leaving my home and family would have to be the first step toward achieving that goal.

By the time I was thirteen years old, I had had enough of school. I had already seen my two brothers leave home to begin their culinary trade. I was too much of a free spirit to be confined to the routine of school, so I dropped out. My parents, of course, did not approve, but they realized I was determined to learn the trade of a chef. In 1934 with the help of my aunt and uncle—who were well connected in the restaurant business in Grenoble—I was able to begin my apprenticeship at the Restaurant Phillipe, which was under the ownership of Claudius Phillipe Sr. Claudius had been a chef in London, Paris and Russia, and was well known throughout France. As an aside, I must point out that I owe much of my success to the Phillipe family, for it was after my apprenticeship that Claudius' son, Claudius Phillipe Jr., asked me to come to the United States and work as saucier at the Waldorf-Astoria, where he was a director.

I was very eager to begin learning my trade, though my enthusiasm would soon be tempered by intermittent bouts of homesickness. It was hard to be away from home. At times, after work, I would actually sit alone in my room and cry. But in the morning I looked forward to going to work and trading gibes with the other men in the kitchen. Eventually, I worked through my sense of dislocation and gained more and more confidence in my cooking skills. I have always been an independent soul—a survivor—and I can remember telling my papa during one of his visits, "I am going to make it in this life!"

Our training was rigorous. We worked seven days a week, usually from 7:30 in the morning to 10:30 at night. Since in those days there was no gas or electricity to cook with, we would begin by cleaning out the ashes from the previous day and restarting the stoves with new coals. After this tiresome chore we would travel with the chefs to the market. At the time the wholesale merchants, such as the fish vendors and meat vendors, did not make door-to-door deliveries to all the restaurants, as is the case today. It was the responsibility of the kitchen crew to go to the city's marketplace each day and obtain the needed supplies. Claudius would usually apprise one of the chefs of what was needed for the day's menu, and the apprentices would go along to learn about the marketing. And, of course, to help carry the supplies back to the restaurant.

To a young apprentice such as I, the sights and sounds of the market were fascinating. This was where aii the deals were made between the chefs and vendors. If an apprentice wanted to become a good chef he would first have to learn how to discriminate between good produce and not-so-good produce. And once he learned that, how to negotiate a fair price. For a chef, the price paid for an item was a crucial factor, because that price would determine the item's eventual selling price in the restaurant. The competition was often fierce between vendors and chefs. The chefs always had two or three merchants that they would regularly buy from. If a chef was not satisfied with the unit price he would tell them, "Too high." The three vendors would retort with an argument; the chef would always try to hold out until one of the vendors was willing to make a deal. I learned an enormous amount of kitchen savvy from these exchanges.

The goods available at the market were not much different from those of today. However, the presentation truly was. In my time, for example, if you bought a pheasant, chicken or rabbit from a vendor, the animal was always alive. Today, if you purchase one of these animals at a market it will no doubt be dead, cleaned, deskinned and even cut into different sections. Likewise the fish. In my time the fish, whether it was turbot, monkfish or striped bass, were often alive when you bought them. Today, these fish are gutted, scaled and already cut into fillets when they are purchased from the merchant. Meat vending has changed as well. Back then the meat was not cut up into pretty little packages marked rump steak, entrecôte, or flank steak, as we see today. On the contrary, what you bought from a butcher would be in large sections, such as an entire leg of lamb or beef. Though the range of market goods has not changed much from my time—because French food has not changed—today's vendors and suppliers have made the preparation and presentation of goods significantly easier for chefs.

The Grenoble market also provided a great meeting place for apprentices employed at restaurants throughout the city. Stories of personal experiences were shared, and there was frequent gossip about mean chefs who had mistreated their subordinates. Against this backdrop of gossiping voices could be heard the animated rush and sounds of animals and the pitched voices of buying and selling. It reminded me of a carnival.

From the market we would return to the restaurant and begin cleaning the produce. This was not always as easy as one might expect. Learning to prepare fish, by scaling it and cleaning the insides, was generally straightforward when compared to preparing eels. As the eels were lifted from a bucket they had a tendency to slip away or wrap themselves around your hand. Eventually, you would resign yourself to the situation by biting into one end to hold it still, and then skinning it with your hands. Defeathering poultry was fairly simple, but only after the just-decapitated birds stopped their grisly and bizarre dancing. Fortunately, fresh vegetables, after they are cleaned and cut, don't behave much differently from when you buy them.

As one can see, the learning process was quite complete and, between meals, extended to cleaning the floors, range, pots and pans. This was truly our baptism.

An inevitable element of this rite of passage was the practical jokes played on us by the older chefs. Two such incidents stand out clearly in my memory. On one occasion one of the chefs said to me, "Hey, Petit, take the pestle and mash up some cork and vinegar in the mortar." Although it sounded strange to me, I really didn't know any better, and so I started to mash the cork and vinegar as I was told. My eyes soon began to tear from the fumes of the vinegar, and my arms grew weak from trying to mash the cork. One of the chefs saw what was going on and, after some time, told me that that was enough. I felt quite silly afterward, but then you never questioned your teacher. You just did as you were told.

On another occasion one of the older chefs instructed me to take a bag over to one of the nearby restaurants. As I went to lift the bag I could not believe how heavy it was. Still, I did not question what was inside. Slowly dragging this heavy bag—which had to weigh more than I did—through the streets of Grenoble, I eventually arrived at the restaurant. The chef there continued to play out the joke, instructing me to take the bag to still another restaurant. Finally, upon arriving at the second restaurant, and quite exhausted at this point, I was told by the chef there that I was the subject of a practical joke and should return to the Restaurant Phillipe. As it turned out, the bag was filled with heavy cast-iron stove plates.

I also remember the day one of my fellow apprentices decided to make a nuisance of himself. The chef said that if he didn't stop, he would let him have it with a two-pronged fork in the derrière. The chef was only joking, but he made a movement to illustrate his point. As he advanced, the apprentice moved out of the way and I got the fork right in my rear. Well, I let out one hell of a sound. I've still got the marks to prove it.

The older chefs would somehow always find fault with something you did and make you stay after work. I remember one such time, when I was told to stay and clean the kitchen and *all* the pots and pans. I began washing the pots and came across one that looked as if it contained dirty water. Not giving the water a second thought, I proceeded to dump it out.

The next morning, one of the chefs came in to see about the consommé he had prepared the night before. As he approached the stove he asked a group of us standing there, "Where is the consommé?" None of us knew what he was talking about. He then called to me, "Hey, Petit, did you clean the kitchen last night?" I answered, "Yes." He again asked about the consommé. Then it dawned on me that he was referring to the dirty water. So I said, "You mean the dirty water inside that pot I cleaned?" I had thrown out the consommé, which had not clarified yet. Where I came from, consommé was called "bouillon," and so I had not understood right away. I had expected an angry reaction, but to my amazement, the chef didn't yell at all. Mistakes were acceptable, so long as we learned from them.

The next step in our training, after learning about preparation, was to begin rotating between the various stations in the kitchen. The positions and responsibilities of each man in the kitchen were well defined. The hierarchy resembled that of a president and his cabinet. At the top of the hierarchy was Claudius, since he was both the executive chef and owner. As the executive chef he was responsible for creating the menu each day, deciding what would be purchased at the market and overseeing all kitchen activity. As we apprentices would say to one another, he was God on earth.

Under the executive chef was the *sous chef*. He was the right-hand man to Claudius, and his basic responsibility was to make sure that anything Claudius wanted done *was* done. He would be in charge of running the kitchen and calling the orders if Claudius was away or had stepped out of the kitchen to say hello to some clients. The sous chef did most of the dirty work and made sure every member of the crew was doing what they should.

Reporting to the sous chef were the *chefs de partie* (chefs of the party), each of whom headed a particular station. Their titles and duties were, respectively: 1) *saucier* (sauce cook), responsible for preparation of all the sauces for meats and stocks, sautéing the veal and chicken and braising the meats; 2) *entremetier* (vegetable cook), responsible for the garnish, soups, omelettes and, of course, all the vegetable preparation; 3) *poissonnier* (fish cook), responsible for cooking all the fish, such as turbot, sole and bass, as well as preparing the fish sauces, such as beurre blanc (white butter), Hollandaise and sauce vin blanc (white wine sauce); 4) *rôtisseur* (roast cook), responsible for broiling fish, roasting meats, poultry and game, and making all the fried food as well as pomme frits (french fries); 5) *garde-manger* (cold food cook), responsible for the preparation of the cold dishes such as pâtés, as well as the vegetables to be used to decorate each dish; 6) *patissier* (pastry chef), responsible for the creation and preparation of all the desserts; 7) *boucher* (butcher), responsible for the carving of all the cuts of veal, beef, lamb, poultry and game; 8) *chef tournant* (turning chef), a very important man indeed, responsible for filling in for any of the other chefs de partie on their days off. The chef tournant knew each station so well that he could change position at a moment's notice to make up for a missing saucier, entremetier or poissonnier.

Each chef de partie had maybe three or four *commis* (assistants) working for him. Many times, when dinner was being served, there were well over thirty-three men working in the kitchen. Though the structure of today's kitchens has remained intact, the number of personnel has been reduced because the overhead is just too great.

As an apprentice I would move every three months to a new station, continuing to rotate until I had learned the particular skills and responsibilities of each position. The learning process was always the same. We would first watch the way the chef did it, and then practice what we were taught as the chef looked on. For example, the garde-manger would show us how to peel and carve the vegetables into decorative creations, then we would try to carve the vegetables in the same way. Once the chef was satisfied that we'd performed the function properly, we'd move to another station. This was the process by which we were taught. It was trial and error, then practice, practice, practice. We learned every basic function of cooking, from how to carve the meat off the bone, to how to make the sauce, to how to decorate the dish. Although French chefs often become masters of one station, finding themselves most comfortable as pastry chef, poissonnier or saucier, the reason they're credited as being among the world's greatest chefs is that they have a mastery of each function performed in the kitchen.

Not all the apprentices I trained with were able to handle the pressure. The world of the kitchen is unique. The hours are long and exhausting, and there is no escape from the sweltering heat, which one cannot fully understand unless he's been in a kitchen all day. Adding to the stress is the lack of an offsetting social life. Back then, we worked from early morning far into the evening, often with only an hour-and-a-half break in the afternoon, if we were lucky enough not to get cleaning duty. When work was over, all we really wanted to do was sleep. There wasn't much entertainment we could avail ourselves of anyway, since we weren't getting paid. To become a chef took an awful lot of dedication and discipline, and a willingness to sacrifice much of one's waking time to his craft. One had to love the life to endure it. We were only thirteen and fourteen years old but were forced by the nature of the trade to forego many of the things kids our age would have enjoyed.

Undoubtedly, one of the greatest hardships we suffered was not being able to visit much with our families. I remember with sadness those occasions when my maman would travel from Rives to drop off clothes or to give me a couple of francs. We were so busy in the kitchen that I could not even leave to spend time with her. She would come to the screen door in the back of the restaurant, and I would just touch her hand through the wire screen. I couldn't even kiss her. She often had to leave quickly, since she had to catch a train to get back home. I hold no bitterness or reproach, but this is how it was.

Many apprentices left early in their training because of the demands placed on them. The pressure to perform, and perform well, while being monitored by one's teacher through lunch and dinner, was ever-present. There was very little in the way of glory or reward, and only an occasional word of encouragement. But deep down I knew I wanted to be a chef. I was very aware of the rich tradition associated with French cuisine, and I wanted to contribute, however humbly, to that tradition. I was always very ambitious. I did not come from a monied background, but my mother and father had instilled in me a deep sense of pride and a will to succeed that became my driving force.

During my years as an apprentice the station that most appealed to me was, without question, the saucier's, for it was at that station that I excelled. I showed a special aptitude for preparing classic French sauces such as béarnaise, béchamel, Hollandaise, fond brun (brown sauce) and others. With great passion I made them to just the right consistency, taste and delicateness. I was able to work with the saucier for the final eight months of my apprenticeship. Sensing my enthusiasm and natural ability, my teacher told Claudius it would be good for me to learn all I could about the station before I graduated. The art of making sauces is a delicate one because so much depends on the taste. The saucier must have an acute sense of taste, always making sure that his sauce is not too salty, not too bitter, not too light, not too heavy. It is an art of the most subtle balances. Like the chemist, the saucier concocts, modifies and redefines his recipe, then offers it to the public for response. In French cuisine the sauce must always complement the food, never overpower it. I think it is this challenge of taste and balances that most attracted me to the craft of sauce making.

After two years of apprenticeship. it was clear to Claudius that I was ready to move on. To do so required that I pass a test, a mark of completion that would display the sum total of all my knowledge. It would actually combine the rigor of all my experiences.

In France, a test is mandatory to complete an apprenticeship. A group of chefs from the many restaurants in Grenoble would convene in a restaurant kitchen and one of them would call out an order to you, such as *sole au beurre blanc* (poached sole with white butter) and *gratin Dauphinois* (potatoes au gratin Dauphin style). You were also to prepare an appetizer, entreé, vegetable and dessert. All of the necessary ingredients for the dishes were at hand; yet you never knew what you were making beforehand, so it was necessary to have the recipe for everything in your head. The pressure was truly enormous, since the chefs would be able to tell right away if you didn't know what you were doing. Even so, when I arrived for the test and began making the dishes, I felt confident that I was going to make it. I was prepared, and I was in the kitchen—a place that always made me feel at ease. Though I did ask myself more than once, "If I *don't* pass this test, what will my father say?" there were very few jitters.

Once I passed the test I was faced with the decision of where to go next to improve my skills. There was still so much to learn. Claudius had valuable connections all over France, and he presented me with three options: I could continue to work in Grenoble, I could go to Nice and work at the Hotel Negresco or I could go to the Hotel Raphael in Paris. For me, Paris was the magic word. It was a decision that I'll never regret.

The one thing that still stands out in my mind about my last day in Grenoble was what Claudius gave me before I boarded the train. He presented me with my certificate of apprenticeship, six toques, six pairs of kitchen pants, six kitchen vests and a ticket to Paris. He then shook my hand and said, *"Bonne chance, Jean."* Good luck. I was on my way.

APPETIZERS

Chilled Vichyssoise
LEEK AND POTATO SOUP

1 lb. potatoes, peeled and thinly sliced
4 oz. onions, sliced thin
4 oz. white part of leeks, thinly sliced
1 teaspoon finely chopped shallots
1 bay leaf
6 cups chicken broth
1 pint heavy cream (very cold)
1 pint milk (very cold)
1 teaspoon finely chopped chives
Salt and freshly ground pepper to taste

1. Combine potatoes, onions, leeks, chopped shallots, bay leaf and chicken stock in soup pot. Simmer covered, until thoroughly cooked. Remove bay leaf.

2. Put through fine mill and cool.

3. Add the cold heavy cream and milk to the soup, season to taste. Sprinkle with chopped chives before serving.

SERVES 6

NOTE: If any graininess still exists from potatoes, soup may be put through a very fine strainer before adding chives.
Soup should be served in chilled cups.
The base may be prepared and stored under refrigeration, adding heavy cream, milk, and chives just before serving. The base, without cream and milk should keep for several days if properly refrigerated.

Les Endives Tombées
BRAISED ENDIVE

1¼ lbs. unblemished Belgian endive, about 8 to 10
3 tablespoons butter
Salt and freshly ground pepper to taste
¼ teaspoon sugar

1. Trim off the base of each endive. Cut the endive on the bias into 1-inch lengths. There should be just about 2 cups.

2. Grease a heavy casserole with the butter and sprinkle with salt and pepper to taste and sugar.

3. Add the endive and salt to taste. Cook about 5 minutes, stirring often. Cover and cook about 6 to 8 minutes more.

SERVES 4

ENTRÉES

Navarin D'Agneau
LAMB STEW

1¾ lb. lamb, cut from the leg in 1½-in. cubes
2 tablespoons butter
1 large onion, chopped,
3 cloves garlic, peeled and crushed
1 tablespoon flour
3 cups beef broth or consommé
   Salt and freshly ground pepper to taste
1 large bay leaf
   Pinch of dried thyme
1 lb. potatoes, peeled and diced into 1½-in. cubes
1½ cups of carrots, cut into sticks
1 cup small white onions, peeled
1 cup white turnips, cut 1½ ins. long
1 cup frozen baby peas
3 tomatoes, peeled and diced
   Chopped parsley

1. Brown the meat on all sides in 2 tablespoons of butter in a hot skillet. Transfer to a heavy kettle.

2. Add the onions and garlic to the meat and sauté for 2 minutes on medium heat. Sprinkle with flour, mix well, and cook again for 2 minutes. Add the broth, salt, pepper, bay leaf, and thyme. Bring to a boil and cover. Boil slowly for half an hour. Add potatoes, carrots, onions, and turnips, and let that cook for 25 minutes until the meat is tender and vegetables are done.

3. Add peas and tomatoes and cook for 5 more minutes. Serve sprinkled with chopped parsley.

SERVES 6

Royal Squab Diable Crapaudine (Pigeonneau)

1 royal squab (pigeon, available at fine butcher
   shops)
Salt and freshly ground black pepper to taste
1 tablespoon melted butter
1 teaspoon imported Dijon mustard
2 drops Tabasco sauce
2 tablespoons fresh white bread crumbs

1. Split the squab horizontally, from the tip of the breast to the wing. Flatten slightly. Season with salt and pepper. Spread with half of the melted butter and let it cook on the grill.

2. Brush the squab with mustard, to which Tabasco has been added. Coat with bread crumbs. Sprinkle with remaining melted butter. Finish cooking the squab on the grill at a low heat, until bread crumbs are golden brown.

3. Set the squab on a round dish. Garnish with a bouquet of watercress and potato chips, and serve with Sauce Diable (see page 121).

SERVES 1

NOTE: Baby chicken, cornish hen, or pigs feet may be substituted for Royal Squab or Pigeonneau. Serve with Gratin Dauphinois (see page 27).

Gratin Dauphinois
CREAM POTATOES AU GRATIN

1 lb. Idaho potatoes, peeled
1½ cups milk, scalded
2 cloves garlic
Salt and white pepper to taste
2 tablespoons butter
¾ cup heavy or light cream

1. Slice potatoes finely. Put them in a bowl and moisten with a mixture of boiled milk and one clove of garlic.

2. Season with salt and pepper to taste.

3. Using 1 tablespoon of butter, grease a 1-quart baking dish and rub with 1 clove of garlic. Put the potato mixture into the buttered dish.

4. Bake at 350°F for half an hour.

5. Add the heavy or light cream and scatter 1 tablespoon of butter, in tiny pieces, over the top. Bake for another 15 minutes at 300°F, until top becomes golden brown. Serve in the dish in which the potatoes are cooked.

SERVES 4

Blanquette de Veau
VEAL IN CREAM SAUCE

4 lbs. boneless shoulder of veal (cut into 2-in.-square
    pieces)
8 cups beef broth
   Salt and freshly ground white pepper to taste
2 whole cleaned carrots
1 medium onion studded with a clove
1 celery stalk
1 leek
1 bouquet garni (thyme, bay leaf, parsley, and a
    garlic clove tied together in cheesecloth)
3 tablespoons butter
3 tablespoons flour
24 peeled small white onions
½ lb. small mushrooms
1 cup heavy cream
2 egg yolks
   Juice of ½ lemon
   Chopped parsley

1. Put the meat in a deep kettle and cover with water. Bring to a boil. Drain the meat, setting the broth aside, and run under cold water until the meat is cold.

2. Return the meat to the kettle and cover with the broth. Add salt, pepper, carrot, onion with clove, celery, leek, and bouquet garni. Simmer gently for about 1 hour until meat is tender. Set aside.

3. Drain cooking liquid from the kettle, and set aside. discard the vegetables and bouquet garni. Remove meat from kettle and set aside.

4. In the kettle, heat the butter and flour and mix with a wire whisk for a couple of minutes. Add the liquid and small onions. Let this simmer gently for 5 minutes. Add meat and mushrooms. Let simmer for another minute.

5. In a bowl mix heavy cream and egg yolks with a wire whisk. Blend this mixture into the veal, stirring until the sauce starts to boil. Add lemon juice and chopped parsley, correct the seasoning, and serve with rice pilaf, buttered noodles, or Navets Anna (see below).

SERVES 8 TO 10

NOTE: Garnish with heart-shaped croutons, fried in butter, if desired.

Navets Anna

TURNIPS MOLDED IN BUTTER

6 medium-size white turnips, about 1½ lbs.
5 tablespoons butter
   Salt and freshly ground pepper

1. Preheat the oven to 400°F.

2. Peel the turnips and, using a vegetable slicer, cut them into slices about ⅛ inch thick. There should be about 4 cups.

3. Heat 4 tablespoons butter in a skillet; add the turnip slices. Sprinkle with salt and pepper to taste. Cook over moderate heat, turning the slices gently, taking care they do not break. Cook about 10 minutes or until slices are slightly limp and translucent.

4. Rub a round cake tin (9¼ by 1½ ins.) with one tablespoon of butter. Arrange the slices over the pan and place in oven. Bake 15 minutes. Cover closely with a lid that will sit inside the pan, directly on top of the turnip slices. Cook 15 minutes.

5. Uncover and cook 25 to 30 minutes longer.

SERVES 6

Gougonnettes of Sole

2 filets sole or flounder
⅓ cup milk
⅓ cup flour
3–5 cups vegetable oil
½ bunch parsley
Salt to taste

1. Cut the filets in long strips, about ¼ inch wide by 4 inches long.

2. Place the fish strips in a soup plate. Cover with milk; lift the pieces of fish from the milk and dip them into the flour, shaking off the excess.

3. Heat the vegetable oil to 375° F. Dip Gougonnettes, a handful at a time, into the oil. Fry for 5 minutes, or until evenly golden brown.

4. Lift the Gougonnettes from the oil with a slotted spoon and drain in a pan lined with paper towels. Sprinkle lightly with salt.

5. Arrange on a platter with lemon wedges and fried parsley.

SERVES 2

NOTE: Serve with Mustard Sauce (see page 34), Lobster Sauce (see page 222) or Tomato Sauce (see page 36).

Coquille St. Jaques

2 cups bay scallops (or sea scallops cut ½ in. thick)
½ cup Fish Broth (see page 68)
½ cup dry white wine
1 shallot, finely chopped
  Salt and freshly ground white pepper to taste
1 tablespoon butter
1 tablespoon flour
⅓ cup heavy cream
1 egg yolk
  Juice of half a lemon
  Dash of Tabasco Sauce
2 tablespoons Hollandaise Sauce (see page 32)
  Chopped parsley

1. Combine scallops with fish broth, wine, shallot, salt, and pepper in a small saucepan and bring to a boil. Cover and simmer for 1 minute. Drain the broth and set aside.

2. Melt 1 tablespoon of butter and stir the flour in with a wire whisk. When blended, add reserved broth and cream, stirring with the whisk.

3. Remove sauce from the heat and mix in the egg yolk, lemon juice, Tabasco, Hollandaise, and chopped parsley.

4. Spoon a little of the sauce into 4 scallop shells. Top with equal portions of scallops. Cover with the remaining sauce.

5. Glaze under the broiler until golden brown.

SERVES 2

SAUCES

Hollandaise Sauce

2 egg yolks
1 tablespoon water
¾ cup melted butter
Few drops of lemon juice
Pinch of salt
Pinch of white pepper
Pinch of cayenne pepper

1. Combine egg yolks and water in top of double boiler. Blend constantly with a wire whisk over hot (not boiling) water until yolks thicken to consistency of cream. Add melted butter a spoonful at a time, beating continually until sauce is thickened.

2. If sauce is too firm, correct consistency by adding warm water. Complete sauce by adding drops of lemon juice, salt, white pepper, and cayenne.

SERVES 4

NOTE: Use sauce for asparagus, broccoli, cauliflower, string beans, or artichokes. Delicious as a glaze for baked or broiled fish, poached fish, poached eggs, or Eggs Benedict.

Béarnaise Sauce

1 teaspoon chopped shallots
1 tablespoon chopped tarragon
1½ tablespoons white vinegar
Pinch of freshly ground black pepper
Pinch of salt
1 tablespoon cold water

32

2 egg yolks
¾ cup melted butter
1 speck cayenne pepper

1. In a small saucepan, combine the shallots, half the tarragon, vinegar, black pepper, and salt. Reduce this mixture by half, remove from heat, and stir in the egg yolks and cold water.

2. Place the sauce pan in the top of a double boiler over hot (not boiling) water. With a wire whisk, stir the mixture constantly until the yolks thicken and have the consistency of cream.

3. Continuing to beat, add the melted butter, a spoonful at a time. Add the remaining tarragon and the cayenne pepper, serve with broiled meat or fish.

YIELDS 1 CUP

Beurre Blanc
WHITE BUTTER SAUCE

2 tablespoons finely chopped shallots
2 tablespoons red wine vinegar
2 tablespoons dry white wine
1 tablespoon water
2 tablespoons heavy cream
½ lb. butter at room temperature
Salt and white pepper to taste

1. Combine shallots, vinegar, white wine, and water in a saucepan and bring to a boil. Cook until most of the liquid has evaporated. Add the heavy cream and bring to a boil.

2. Add the butter bit by bit, stirring rapidly with a wire whisk over moderate heat. Boil gently until the sauce is thickened and creamy. Season with salt and white pepper to taste.

YIELDS ABOUT 1 CUP

NOTE: Can be used with any fish mousse, poached fish, broiled shrimp, lobster, or scallops.

Mustard Sauce

2 egg yolks
1 tablespoon water
¾ cup melted butter
1 tablespoon Dijon mustard
Few drops of lemon juice
Pinch of salt
1 tablespoon chopped chives
Dash of Tabasco
Pinch of white pepper
Pinch of cayenne pepper

1. Combine the egg yolks and water in top of double broiler. Blend and work with wire whisk over hot (not boiling) water until yolks thicken to consistency of cream.

2. Add the melted butter a spoonful at a time, then add mustard, beating continually until sauce is thickened. If sauce is too firm, correct consistency by adding warm water.

3. Complete sauce by adding drops of lemon juice, salt, chives, Tabasco, and white and cayenne peppers.

SERVES 4

NOTE: You can use this sauce for Royal Squab (see page 26), and any broiled meats such as beef, veal, lamb, pork and poultry, and fish.

Sauce Vin Blanc
WHITE WINE SAUCE

4 tablespoons butter
3 tablespoons flour
3 cups Fish Broth (see page 68)
    Salt and freshly ground white pepper to taste
    Pinch of Cayenne pepper
½ cup chopped mushrooms
½ cups heavy cream
1 tablespoon lemon juice

1. Heat 3 tablespoons of butter in a saucepan. Add flour, mixing with a wire whisk. Add fish broth, stirring rapidly with whisk.

2. When the sauce has thickened and smoothed, add salt, pepper, cayenne, and mushrooms. Cook for 10 to 15 minutes.

3. Add cream to sauce and cook 3 to 5 minutes until sauce reduces to about 4 cups. Put sauce through fine china cap or fine sieve— press to extract as much as possible.

4. Pour sauce into saucepan and bring to boil. Add lemon juice and remaining butter, and serve.

YIELDS 4 CUPS

NOTE: You can add 1 tablespoon per serving Hollandaise Sauce (see page 32) for a richer and smoother sauce.

Sauce Tomate

1 small chopped onion
2 cloves garlic, finely chopped
3 tablespoons butter
1 tablespoon flour
2 cups crushed fresh tomatoes
1 small can tomato paste
2 cups beef broth
1 small bay leaf
  Pinch of dried thyme
  Pinch of oregano
  Pinch of dried basil or 1 teaspoon chopped fresh basil
  Salt and freshly ground pepper to taste

1. In a saucepan, sauté onions and garlic with 2 tablespoons of butter for 2 minutes. Sprinkle with flour, stirring to blend well.

2. Add the tomatoes, tomato paste, beef broth, bay leaf, thyme, oregano, basil, salt and pepper. Cook gently, stirring occasionally for 15 to 20 minutes.

3. Strain the entire mixture through china cap or fine sieve into a saucepan, pressing with a wooden pestle or spoon.

4. Heat the sauce to a boil and add 1 tablespoon of butter.

YIELDS 3 CUPS

NOTE: This is an excellent sauce for any pasta or Gougonnettes of Sole or Flounder (see page 30)

DESSERTS

Bread and Custard Pudding

2½ cups milk
1 cup heavy cream
¼ cup butter
8 thin slices French bread, toasted
½ cup sugar
3 eggs, lightly beaten
¼ cup cognac
1 teaspoon cinnamon
½ cup seedless raisins

1. Preheat oven to 375° F.

2. Scald the milk and cream. Add the butter and pour the hot liquid over the bread. Soak for about 5 minutes. Then add sugar, eggs, cognac, cinnamon, and raisins, and stir.

3. Pour the mixture into a butter baking dish. Set the dish in a pan of hot water and bake until a knife inserted in the center comes out clean, about 45 minutes.

SERVES 4 TO 6

Crêpes

¾ cup sifted flour
6 eggs
1 quart milk
2 teaspoons sugar
   Pinch of salt
¼ cup butter

1. Mix the flour and eggs with a wire whisk. Add the milk, sugar, and salt, and beat until the ingredients are thoroughly blended.

2. Melt the butter in a small pan and skim off the foam. Pour off and reserve the clarified portion. Discard the sediment in the bottom of the pan.

3. Heat a 4-in. skillet and brush it with the clarified butter. Pour in 1 tablespoon of the batter and tilt the pan immediately so that the batter will spread over the entire bottom of the pan. Cook the crêpe quickly on both sides.

4. Repeat the process until all the crêpes are cooked, stacking them on a plate as they are finished. If the crêpes are to be sauced later, cover with wax paper to prevent drying.

YIELDS 20 CRÊPES

Crêpes Suzette

4 lumps sugar
1 orange
  Few drops lemon
½ cup butter
 1 jigger (3 tablespoons) maraschino
 1 jigger (3 tablespoons) curaçao
 1 jigger (3 tablespoons) kirsch
 3 crêpes per serving (see page 38)

1. Rub the lumps of sugar on the orange skin until they are covered with the aromatic oil. Squeeze the orange and reserve the juice.

2. Crush the sugar with half the butter and cream well.

3. Place the rest of the butter in a flat skillet or a chafing dish over low heat and when it melts add the creamed butter, orange and lemon juice, marachino, and curaçao, and stir with a wooden spoon until well blended. Add the kirsch and ignite. Keep the sauce barely simmering over a spirit lamp or other low flame.

4. Add the crêpes one at a time and, using a fork and large spoon, turn each crêpe over in the sauce, then fold into quarters. Serve very hot.

SERVES 4 TO 6

The kitchen staff at the Hotel Royal, 1949. I'm seated in the first row, far right.

III

JOURNEYMANSHIP

Paris in the late 1930s and early '40s was full of beauty and excitement. I arrived in the city, at the age of sixteen, with the wide eyes and great expectations common to most country boys and set out immediately, just as any tourist would, to visit the sites I had heard talked about all my life. I went to such places as the Eiffel Tower, Notre-Dame de Paris, the Arc de Triomphe and Montmartre. It was all so impressive. The only city I had known before Paris was Grenoble, but judged against the sprawling grandeur of France's capital, Grenoble seemed like a small town.

The nightlife was particularly exciting. After my work was finished I would get together with my brothers, Roger and Lucien, who were also working in Paris at the time, and other friends and make the rounds of nightclubs and cabarets. We did what young men do, meeting girls, talking with them and inviting them to dance. There was much singing as well, which had us up until the early hours of the morning. It was a heady existence for a sixteen-year-old far from home. Looking back, I think we were a little bit crazy.

I had the privilege of continuing my education at the Hotel Raphael, one of the finest *grand luxe* hotel restaurants in Paris at the time, and which today is still located on the Avenue Kleber near the Arc de Triomphe. There I began my training as an assistant to the entremetier and was in charge of preparing all the vegetables, garnishes and soups. However, I did not remain at this station for long. The chefs in charge moved me around often, so that I could sharpen the skills I had learned as an apprentice. Within weeks I was moved to the garde-manger station, where I was responsible for assisting in the preparation of all the cold foods, such as buffet dishes and pâtés. After serving at the garde-manger station I became an assistant to the rôtisseur, and then to the poissonnier.

One must realize that although I had completed my apprenticeship, the training I was receiving at the Hotel Raphael was an extension of my apprenticeship. I was still very much a commis, and would be for several more years. Once I had learned enough I could then head my own station and become a chef de partie, such as a saucier, rotisseur, and so on. But I had some ripening to do first.

It was while working for the poissonnier, Henri Beck, that the chefs realized I excelled in the preparation of sauces. Henri told Charles Lecas, the saucier, how well I was doing in preparing the fish sauces and suggested that it might be wise for me to move to the saucier station. Charles then asked the executive chef, Egem Burger, if I could be his assistant, because nothing is done without the approval of the executive chef. Before I knew it I was working under Charles' supervision and doing the thing I liked best: preparing sauces.

Though Henri Beck, Charles Lecas and Egem Burger are not household names, especially in America, these were very important men whom I, and many others, came to idolize. They were all chefs, and all were members of L'Académie de Culinaire de France—one of France's most elite societies and one whose members had to be selected. These men, most especially Charles Lecas, had great influence on my development. To have such masters teaching me made all the difference in the world.

As the months passed, Charles gave me more and more opportunity to produce the classic French sauces. Under his guidance I was making *sauce espagnole* (brown sauce), Hollandaise, béchemal, béarnaise, and *fond brun de volaille* (brown chicken sauce), to name a few. I did not try to experiment when making these sauces. At this stage in my development the idea was to first reproduce these classic recipes to the best of my ability. There would be plenty of time later in my career for experimenting and changing. As is true of any art form, one cannot experiment properly if one has not yet even learned the basics of the tradition. I still remember the first time Charles allowed the sauce I had prepared to be served. I had made a brown sauce in the afternoon and let it sit over a low flame for most of the day, mixing it occasionally so it would not stick to the pan. By dinner it was tasting delicious, if I may say so myself. When an order for veal marsala was called that required the brown sauce I'd made, Charles asked me to hand the pot over to him. He took one taste of the sauce with his finger and said, "Serve it." Not historic words, I grant you, but I was most relieved.

During the time I was working at the Hotel Raphael I was making some money, but by no means a lot. Since going out at night was expensive, I found a few small ways to supplement my income. As an assistant it was my responsibility to come in early to begin the preparation for lunch. While preparing the Hollandaise sauce I would take about two dozen egg whites, which I had separated from the yolks, and set them aside. During my break, which was usually from 3:30 to 5:00 P.M., I would take the egg whites and sell them to one of the pastry shops for a few francs. I would also take a portion of the *glaze de viande* (meat glaze), a concentrated beef-based glaze used to enhance sauces and stews, and sell it to the *charcuteries* (delicatessens). I was never caught outright taking these things, but I think it was something the chefs knew about, but overlooked, realizing I was only trying to make some extra money. I also think the chefs probably had done the same things when they were in my position.

I remained at the Hotel Raphael as an assistant to Charles until 1941, when the Germans seized Paris and sent me, along with thousands of other Frenchmen, to work in the mines of Longwy (Lorraine) as part of the S.T.O. (Service de Travaille Obligatoire) program. One day we were literally picked up off the streets and herded onto trains, with no questions asked. I spent two long years as a prisoner of war. Although the war is something I would prefer not to discuss at length, I bring it up because I believe it was my ability as a chef that saved my life.

As the Allies began advancing into France, the Germans moved us further east toward the German border. I made two attempts to escape. The first time, when I was captured I was asked, "What were you trying to do?" I replied, "As long as I am a prisoner I will try to do what I am obligated to do—get free." The soldiers who'd apprehended me had been ready to kill me; however, the officers had learned from other prisoners that I knew how to cook. My life was spared, and I was assigned to work in the officers' quarters.

Up until this point, I had always been a free-spirited, positive-minded person. The other prisoners came to rely, I think, on my carefree attitude as a source of hope and inspiration. Yet soon after my thwarted escape attempt, I became visibly distraught. I was weighed down by questions that had never bothered me before: Would I ever get out of here? Would I ever see my family again? Would I ever see *France* again? One day my answer to all of these questions became, emphatically, no. I was prepared to resign myself and let fate run its course.

Fortunately, one of my fellow prisoners, noticing my visible depression, put a challenge to me that completely altered my perspective. He said to me, "Jean, you have always been so full of life since I've been here with you. Are you going to change all that and become like so many of those here who just sit and seem to await death?" His words were like a cold slap on the face. I realized then that to wallow in my depression, like so many others in the camp did, would diminish my chances of survival. Moreover, I would not be living life to the high standards I'd set for myself long ago. From that day on I promised myself I would never again worry about my fate. I would live day by day, each one to the fullest.

It was while working in the kitchen that I was able to successfully escape. One of the German officers, Hans Fisher (a regular soldier, not an SS), had befriended me. One night I went into the kitchen and found that he had left me several German military uniforms hanging up on the coat rack. Along with two other prisoners, we quickly stuffed the clothing into a bag and hid the bag away. One aspect of working in the kitchen was that we had to load a truck with food supplies and drive out to the mines, where some of the prisoners were fed. One day we packed up the truck as usual, but this time we made sure to pack the clothing as well, for this was the day we planned to escape. When we arrived at the mines, which were near the town of Till—fortunately a heavily wooded area—we started unloading the supplies, as we always did. At this point in the war, about 1943, the Germans realized their cause was lost, and since many of the German soldiers were lax, their surveillance was weak. In fact, many prisoners had recently escaped, so I knew that this would be as good a time as any.

When we went back to the truck for more supplies, we grabbed the bag containing the German clothing and quickly put the uniforms on. We wanted to confuse the German guard dogs by wearing German clothing: the dogs would not know our actual scent and would thus be unable to track us. We carefully looked around outside the truck to make sure no soldiers were around. Then, in what seemed like suspended time, we dashed out of the truck and headed for the surrounding woods. We must have run for hours, walking throughout the night with little knowledge of where we were headed. But by early morning, we came upon some French people who offered us some food. It was only then that I knew we had made it.

I eventually found my way back to Verdun, where I joined up with members of the French Resistance until the end of the war. When the war ended, the French government paid me 611 francs—the equivalent of $1.50—for my four years of service, including two years of prison camp. I thought to myself, "I certainly didn't fight in this war for the money."

My movement after the war was both varied and prosperous. The period immediately following the war was one of great readjustment, for me as well as for all of Europe. I returned to Paris in 1944, where I was able to get work at the Hotel Majestic. At this time the Majestic was being used by the American armed forces as their headquarters during the reconstruction of Paris. It was here that I met one of my closest friends, Raymond Richez; he and I would have some great times together. Since the Americans were stationed at the Majestic, they controlled all the food supplies that the army was sending in to feed the soldiers. There was such a surplus of food that the Americans would ask Raymond and me if we could sell some of it for them, since we spoke French and knew the area so well. We were more than happy to oblige because we knew we could take some for ourselves.

I remember one occasion when we were trying to take an entire leg of ham. There was a dumbwaiter in the kitchen, a small air shaft really, into which we threw our supplies. We would call down to another Frenchman who assisted us, and he would yell back up that all was clear. Well, on this particular day Raymond and I were standing with the leg of ham, which must have weighed about fifteen pounds. We thought we heard our cohort say that it was okay, so we tossed the ham down the dumbwaiter. Just as the ham was thrown in, our friend stuck his head in the dumbwaiter and shouted, "Okay, send it down . . . " With those words the leg of ham hit him square in the head and knocked him out. Raymond and I had a good laugh over that one.

Another memorable episode was the time Raymond and I took some eggs that we planned to sell to the pastry shops. Riding on bicycles to the nearby shops, we neared the Place de la Concorde on the Champs Élysées and were met by a barricade of policemen. It was just our luck that that particular day President Charles de Gaulle's motorcade was coming down the Champs Élysées. Raymond and I continued to ride through the barricade. A police officer began blowing his whistle and yelling at us to get out of the way. At that moment my front tire got caught in between the cracks of the cobblestone street, sending me, and the eggs, flying over the bicycle's handlebars. Raymond and I began picking up the eggs that hadn't broken as the policeman continued to shout at us to get out of the way. With the motorcade rapidly approaching, Raymond and I began laughing hysterically. I even remember the policeman putting some of the eggs in his own pockets. It was quite an event.

After a couple of months at the Majestic I decided it was time to get serious and get on with my trade. I went to the Société des Cuisiniers de Paris, which referred qualified members of the trade to select establishments, and managed to obtain the position of saucier at the Restaurant La Cigogne in Paris. I was no longer an assistant but now a chef de partie, which meant I controlled the saucier station and had assistants working for me. Le Cigogne was basically a provincial restaurant, drawing its customers from the Alsatian province of France and serving such foods as fois gras, terrines, pâtés and sausages. It felt good to be working seriously again at my craft. I was content to be heading a station and making steady progress up the professional ladder.

My private life also settled down. In 1945, I married my first wife, Jeannine. I had met her during one of my nightly visits to the cabarets. Jeannine was a hatmaker. She shared my love for the nightlife and dancing that was so much a part of Paris' allure. I loved her very much and tried to provide for her as best I could, but I must admit that my career eventually caused a rupture in the relationship. It was difficult for us because the life of a chef is so demanding. I worked long hours and eventually began moving from one part of the country to the next to pick up more experience. I was not making enough money at the time to think about bringing Jeannine with me. Our distance from each other began to take its toll. It was not until 1950, when I came to America, that I was making some real money and was able to bring her over. But by then our relationship, for all intents and purposes, was finished, and we divorced in 1955.

I left La Cigogne after three months; I was still very much "in training" at this point and the most important thing I could do was broaden my experience. Fortunately, the Société des Cuisiniers de Paris kept me informed of available positions, directing me to such establishments as the Restaurant Le Perigord, Restaurant La Cabaret and Restaurant Lareine Pedauque. I was quite honored that the Société chose to repeatedly consider me. Each of the aforementioned restaurants offered me a slightly different perspective because the menus always differed in some respect. At Le Perigord, for example, the menu offered a lot more variety than at La Cigogne. Le Perigord was a fancy restaurant, rather bourgeois, and catered to the rich clientele of Paris. There, I took the post of garde-manger, in charge of preparing all the cold food dishes such as pâtés, salads and so on. Le Cabaret, which I went to as a poissonnier, in charge of sautéing the fish and preparing the fish sauces, was a restaurant that stressed seafood on its menu. And Lareine Padauque, where I was the saucier, was a legitimate first-class restaurant with a sophisticated clientele and a menu that featured the utmost in French classic cuisine. It was through working at these three restaurants and others like it, in a variety of different positions, that I expanded and refined my knowledge of what might be called the "tricks of the trade." Each dish, no matter how basic, could be prepared in a variety of ways and I knew I'd have to learn all of them if I expected to run my own kitchen one day.

During the seasonal months, the big resort owners from all over

France would come to the Société to ask its executives to arrange for
a group of us to work through the tourist season. Fifty or sixty of us
were chosen, as an elite group, to work in some of the big-name
resorts.

During the winter season I traveled to a prestigious ski resort,
the Hotel Majestic in Chamonix, where I worked as a saucier. During
the spring, I was employed at a famous spa resort, the Hotel Royal,
in Evian, also as a saucier. And during the summer I worked at the
Hotel du Golf in Deauville as a rotisseur. All of these establishments
served as excellent training grounds. The routine was similar from
season to season. The days were spent in the kitchen preparing for
lunch, and after a short break we would return to prepare dinner.
This was not always an easy task when you realize the number of
people we served every night—sometimes as many as five hundred!
Moreover, since many of us in the kitchen never stayed in one place
for more than six months, our training, coordination and efficiency
were all crucial elements. Indeed, in a French kitchen at this time
there were about fifty people performing various tasks in the preparation of the day's menu. This demanded equal amounts of harmony
and discipline between each station and person.

All in all, there was certainly very little time to enjoy myself,
but if you want to become a chef you must certainly be prepared to
sacrifice yourself to the trade. There is very little glory or glamor in
this business. If you are interested in such aspects, I would suggest
you think about working in the dining room as either a maître d' or a
captain. To be frank, the kitchen life is often a thankless one, and
the kind of seasonal work I've just mentioned can have a negative
effect on relationships. It did in my case. I would be gone three
months out of each season. There was no work for Jeannine at these
places, so it was impossible for her to be with me. Yet I had very
little choice but to accept the positions offered me if I was ever to
make something of my life. That was the dilemma I was confronted
with, and at the time I felt there was nothing I could do about it.

After my seasonal excursions I would always return to Paris to
find work in one of the many *grand luxe* restaurants. One afternoon,
while at the Société talking with some of my friends and colleagues
during the break period between lunch and dinner, someone mentioned that a Mr. Christiansen, an auto racer and restauranteur from

Copenhagen, Denmark, was looking to put together a French crew to work at his restaurant, La Belle Terrace. It was located at the European hotspot—Tivoli Gardens. Mr. Christiansen, who loved French food, wanted some of us to come to Denmark to create the food that, as he claimed, "you can find only in France." A few days later one of the Société executives asked me if I would be interested in going to Denmark as the saucier. I did not hesitate for a moment. The thought of traveling had always intrigued me, and this would be the first time I had been outside of France other than during the war. Moreover, being chosen by your peers to represent French culinary culture in another country had to be viewed as an honor when you considered the hundreds who applied for such assignments.

I have fond memories of those times. I quickly learned that my prior stereotyping of the Nordic people as stoic and unfriendly was entirely incorrect. I found them to be most genuinely warm and hospitable. In fact, only a couple of weeks into our tour we were invited by several of the customers to dine at their homes. Because of our language differences, our exchanges were often accomplished through physical gestures more than through conversation, but the overriding sentiment was one of mutual friendship.

La Belle Terrace was the only French restaurant in Denmark, so it had a certain cachet. Its reputation did not suffer from the quality of Denmark's produce, either, which was excellent. The menu was classic French cuisine; from foie gras to ginger soufflés, we provided the customers with a taste of France that I'm sure they greatly enjoyed. I say this because, in the six months of my stay, we were booked solid every night.

One memory that stands out in particular was the time four of the Danish waitresses who worked at La Belle Terrace invited me and a couple of other chefs to go to the beach in Malmo, Sweden, on our day off. Naturally, we jumped at the chance. When we arrived at the beach the chefs and I stripped down to our bathing trunks and headed for the water. As we neared the water, I looked back to see what was taking the girls so long. I stopped in my tracks when I saw that they were completely nude. As they came toward us I tried my best not to stare but failed completely. They were pointing to our shorts as if to say, "Off with them, off with them." People have always said that the French are so liberal and uninhibited. Well, I'll tell you, these girls showed us how puritanical we were. They did finally get us to strip down, but not without some prodding. It was one day off that I can never forget and will never regret.

During the six months I spent at La Belle Terrace as the saucier, a group of us also went to Norway and Sweden to perform culinary demonstrations. All in all, it was a tour rich in both education and personal experience. I have not had a great deal of schooling, but I will always contend that one can learn more about people and culture through travel than from books. Ironically, it has been the success I have achieved as a chef that has allowed me again and again to get "out of my kitchen."

In 1950, after having accumulated a rather extensive résumé, including a stint of almost six years at more than a dozen top restaurants, I was presented with an opportunity that would prove pivotal to my career.

One day, Alfred Guerot, then the administrator of the Société des Cuisiniers de Paris, confided to me that a certain executive chef, Mr. Michaud, was looking to recruit a crew for the opening of the Castle Harbour Hotel in Bermuda. I immediately told Alfred I was interested. I'd always been eager to try something new, and in my mind Bermuda seemed far away and exotic.

Traveling by chartered plane, I was most relieved when we finally arrived. Little did I realize that in less than six months, I would find myself traveling again, but this time bound for America.

At Castle Harbour I occupied the position of chef tournant (turning chef), which meant that I would take the place of the saucier, poissonnier, rôtisseur and entremetier on their days off. By now I had come to understand each station of the kitchen so well that I could stand at any of these positions when called upon. Castle Harbour was a beautiful hotel in the *grand luxe* tradition, and at first Bermuda was everything I had imagined—a paradise. Only after two weeks did I come to realize that nothing can be so boring as living on a small island. One comes to know it like the back of one's hand.

I noticed also that the market goods did not meet the high standard I was accustomed to. A lot of food was imported from Australia and New Zealand. The meat was often frozen, as was the fish. Such things bothered me because I was so used to the freshest of produce and meats at my previous places of employment. There were, however, aspects of Bermuda that I did like. I had much more free time than ever before, so I would often frequent the beach, and I even took up golf. I met a good friend, Marcel Dragon, whom I would eventually bring to The Colony as saucier, and who would later become the executive chef at the Stanford Court Hotel in San Francisco. My brother Roger (later executive chef of the Four Seasons) was also with me in Bermuda. Still, even with these companions I found myself yearning for a change of scenery.

It makes me proud to know that many of the places at which I worked some forty years ago, such as Le Perigord, Hotel Raphael, Hotel Royal, La Belle Terrace and, more recently, the Castle Harbour, are still operating successfully today. That they have stood the test of time is a testament to the way these places are run and the caliber of the men and women who run them.

It was while in Bermuda that I was contacted by Claudius Phillipe Jr., the son of Claudius Sr. with whom I had completed my apprenticeship in Grenoble. Claudius Jr. had learned of my whereabouts from the Société. He had always wanted me to come to the United States, and he told me he was preparing all the necessary papers. At the time he was the director of the famous Waldorf-Astoria Hotel in New York. He asked me if I would be interested in taking the position of saucier at the Waldorf-Astoria Restaurant.

In October of 1950, before I really knew what was happening, I was on the *Queen of Bermuda*, a luxury liner bound for New York City. The trip itself was one long bout of seasickness. My only refreshing recollection is of seeing the Statue of Liberty as we approached the port of New York. To a foreigner seeing it for the first time, it was an impressive sight. I was barely off the ship when I was handed my immigration papers and whisked off in a limousine to meet Claudius at the Waldorf-Astoria. I was bewildered and found it hard to believe that I was actually in a limousine being taken care of like some important person.

My early impressions of New York City were not positive ones. The buildings were enormous, and I kept thinking that they were going to fall on me. The streets were dirty with litter. It all just seemed so big, so different from Paris.

Claudius immediately put me to work as the saucier. I became disenchanted very quickly with what I saw in the kitchen. The

Standing on American soil for the first time. The Queen of Bermuda *is in the background.*

American hotel restaurant system seemed to operate very differently from what I was used to in France. The emphasis on quantity at the Waldorf-Astoria was more extreme than I had ever seen before. The huge quantitites of food that the commercial banquets and buffets demanded was scarcely believable. Although the food was very good, the amount of waste disgusted me.

The entire operation ran contrary to everything I'd ever learned and had been taught to believe. To make matters worse, I was getting pressure from the union, which wanted to know how I was able to become the saucier so quickly when there were union men there who merited my position due to their seniority. Claudius would provide the excuse that these men did not have the background that I had. This situation was something I did not expect, and it made me feel somewhat uncomfortable. The Waldorf-Astoria was just not for me.

Claudius could sense my displeasure but felt that I needed to give my new environs more time. He even told me that George Blanc, the executive chef at the Waldorf-Astoria, was going to retire soon and that I would become executive chef upon his retirement. Yet, I knew that I was not made for such "production." Not that I couldn't handle it. It was just that, at the time, I wanted to work in a position that would allow me to function in such a way that I would gain knowledge applicable to opening my own restaurant. It was important to me that I work in a different type of kitchen operation, but certainly not one that epitomized such sheer efficiency.

I kept telling Claudius that I would rather return to Paris than pursue this upcoming opportunity. I had never planned on staying in America very long to begin with. I wanted to work in a place more in the style of the French kitchen that I was accustomed to. And since I did not speak any English at the time, I found myself unable to communicate in many social situations. Still, Claudius kept telling me to be patient and that he would talk to some people about opportunities at other restaurants. Little did I know that the people he was to contact would have so much impact on my life.

I learned many a lesson during this nomadic period. To a young person interested in becoming a chef, I cannot emphasize enough the importance of movement during one's early years. From 1936, when I arrived in Paris, to 1950, when I came to the Waldorf-Astoria, I had worked in more than a dozen of the world's top restaurants, discharging just about every function possible in the kitchen, with the exception of executive chef.

What I often find disturbing about many of the American chefs who direct this country's better restaurants is that they don't seem to have enough of this journeymanship experience. They may have had a two-year apprenticeship at a culinary institute, but that is not enough. For a person to become a great chef he or she must work at each station in the kitchen and understand how that station functions in respect to all the other stations. In a top restaurant, quality gourmet food is not the creation of one man or woman, but the creative collaboration of several people working together. The American executive chef has talent, to be sure, but many chefs in this country lack the necessary basic experience, exposure and discipline that is such a crucial part of a chef's early training. I tell them this: be patient—learn everything you can about what you are doing before moving on.

APPETIZERS

Chicken Liver Pâté

1 lb. chicken livers
1 medium onion, sliced
1 clove garlic, peeled and crushed
1 bay leaf
Pinch of dried thyme
1 cup water
2 teaspoons salt
1½ cups soft sweet butter
Freshly ground black pepper to taste
1 tablespoon cognac

1. Place the livers, garlic, bay leaf, thyme, water, and 1 teaspoon salt in a saucepan. Bring to a boil and simmer gently for 6 to 8 minutes. Remove from the heat and set the mixture aside for 5 minutes.

2. Remove the solids with a slotted spoon and place them in a food processor. Process the liver, adding the butter piece by piece. Finally, add the second teaspoon of salt, pepper, and cognac, and process for 2 more minutes until the mixture is very creamy and completely smooth.

3. Refrigerate for 12 hours until set.

4. Serve with thin slices of toasted bread or your favorite crackers.

SERVES 12

Tomatoes Farcie Côte D'Azur
STUFFED TOMATOES COTE D'AZUR

½ cup diced cooked shrimp
½ cup lump crabmeat
½ cup diced cooked lobster meat
2 avocadoes, diced
Salt and freshly ground pepper to taste
1 oz. kirsch
2 tablespoons lemon juice
Dash of Tabasco
⅓ cup mayonnaise
¼ cup whipped cream
6 large ripe tomatoes, hollowed and drained
12 large mussels, steamed, in half shells
16 black olives, pitted
2 Granny Smith apples, cut in sections
1 head Boston lettuce
2 cups Celery Root Remoulade (see page 70)
6 large beets, sliced
Bunch of parsley

1. Gently mix shrimp, crabmeat, lobster meat, avocados, salt, pepper, kirsch, lemon juice, and Tabasco. Then add the mayonnaise and whipped cream.

2. Stuff the tomatoes and garnish with 2 mussels in half shells, 1 black olive in the center, and 2 slices of apple on the side.

3. Cover the serving plate with Boston lettuce. Make a bottom with the Celery Root Remoulade. Place the tomatoes in the center of a ring of sliced beet, decorated with small springs of parsley.

SERVES 6

Croquettes of Crabmeat

1 lb. crabmeat
1 cup white bread crumbs
2 eggs
2 tablespoons olive oil
½ cup light cream
2 scallions, coarsely chopped
  Salt and freshly ground black pepper to taste
  Pinch of nutmeg
  Flour for dredging

1. In a large bowl, mix all the ingredients. Make 8 small patties (like hamburgers).

2. Dredge the patties lightly with flour and sauté them in a large skillet with 2 tablespoons of olive oil (or butter) over moderate heat until golden brown on both sides—about 6 minutes.

SERVES 4

NOTE: Serve with Sauce Diable (see page 121) or Lobster Sauce (see page 222).

Quiche Lorraine

6 slices bacon, cut in ¼-in. pieces
1 small onion, finely chopped
2 slices ham, cut in ¼-in. pieces
3 whole eggs plus 2 egg yolks
2 cups heavy cream
  Salt and freshly ground pepper to taste
1 9-in. pie shell
1 cup diced Swiss cheese
1 tablespoon butter, cut in small pieces

1. Preheat oven to 375°F.

2. In a skillet sauté the bacon until crisp, then add the onion and ham and simmer for 2 minutes. Strain fat.

3. In a bowl mix the whole eggs, extra egg yolks, and cream. Add the salt and pepper and beat this mixture with a wire whisk until smooth.

4. Place prebaked pie shell on a baking sheet. Scatter the cheese, bacon, ham, and onions on the bottom of the shell. Then pour the egg mixture into it.

5. Sprinkle the top of the quiche with the butter and bake for about 20 to 25 minutes. (The quiche is done when a knife inserted through the center comes out clean.)

SERVES 6 TO 8

Soufflé au Fromage
CHEESE SOUFFLÉ

3½ tablespoons butter
3 tablespoons flour
1½ cups milk
  Salt and feshly ground pepper to taste
  Pinch of cayenne pepper
6 eggs, separated, plus 2 egg whites
¼ lb. Swiss or Parmesan cheese, grated

1. Preheat oven to 375°F. Butter the inside of a 6-cup soufflé dish with ½ tablespoon of butter.

2. Heat the remaining 3 tablespoons of butter in a saucepan, add the flour, and stir for 1 minute over moderate heat. Stir in the milk with a wire whisk so that it thickens. Let boil for about 10 to 15 seconds, then add the salt, pepper, and cayenne.

3. Reduce the heat to low and add the egg yolks, stirring quickly with a whisk. When the mixture starts to bubble, remove it from the heat and add the cheese, mixing well.

4. Beat the egg whites until stiff and add a third of the egg white to the soufflé mixture. Mix with the whisk, then add the remaining egg whites, folding them in gently with a rubber spatula.

5. Pour soufflé mixture into a soufflé dish and smooth over the top. Bake at 375°F. for approximately 25 minutes.

SERVES 4 TO 6

Delmonico Salad

Recipe of Raymond Richez

½ *head romaine*
½ *head chicory*
½ *head of escarole*
14 *oz. diced chicken*
 2 *avocados, cut in small pieces*
 4 *hard boiled eggs,diced*
12 *strips crips bacon, finely chopped*
½ *bunch watercress*
 2 *tablespoons minced chives*

Tear the romaine, chicory, and escarole into bite-size pieces. Place the lettuces and all remaining ingredients in a bowl and toss throughly. Serve this salad with Roquefort Cream dressing.

SERVES 4 TO 6

Roquefort Cream Dressing

2 *cups French dressing (see page 71)*
4 *tablespoons crumbled Roquefort or blue cheese*
2 *tablespoons cream*

Blend all the ingredients well before serving.

ENTRÉES

Côte de Veau Milanaise
BREADED VEAL CHOP MILANAISE

2 veal chops, pounded thin with a mallet
Salt and freshly ground pepper to taste
1 egg
1 tablespoon vegetable oil
1 cup fresh white bread crumbs
⅓ cup Parmesan cheese
½ cup flour
2 tablespoons butter or vegetable oil

1. Season the flattened veal chops with salt and pepper.

2. Mix the egg with 1 tablespoon of oil. In a separate bowl, mix the bread crumbs and Parmesan. Dredge the veal chops in flour, then in the egg mixture, and then in the bread crumb and cheese mixture.

3. In a large skillet sauté the veal in butter or oil on both sides until cooked to a golden brown, about 3 minutes on each side.

4. Place the meat on 2 warm plates. Garnish with wedges of lemon, a bouquet of watercress, and spaghetti with Tomato Sauce (see page 36).

SERVES 2

Côte de Veau Aplatie
FLATTENED GRILLED VEAL CHOP

1½ lb. veal chop
Salt and freshly ground black pepper to taste
Oil for brushing veal chop
1 teaspoon butter
½ teaspoon chopped parsley
Lemon wedge
Watercress
1 cherry tomato

1. Place the veal chop between sheets of waxed paper and pound it with a flat mallet until it is about ¼ inch thick.

2. Sprinkle meat with salt and pepper, and brush with oil on both sides.

3. Place the flattened veal chop diagonally on a hot grill and cook it about 10 seconds on one side. Give it half a turn on the grill on the same side, and cook 10 seconds more. Turn the flattened veal chop over and cook another 10 seconds. Again, give it a half turn diagonally and cook another 10 seconds. Place veal on a hot plate and place a small amount of butter, mixed with chopped parsley, on top.

4. Garnish with 1 large tablespoon of Gratin Dauphinois (see page 27), the cherry tomato, lemon wedge, and watercress.

SERVES 1

NOTE: This recipe may also be used for Minute Steak Aplatie.

Steak au Poivre à la Creme
PEPPER STEAK WITH CREAM

2 sirloin steaks (about 10 oz. each)
2 teaspoons whole black peppercorns
2 tablespoons butter
2 teaspoons cognac
2 tablespoons Brown Sauce (see page 66)
2 tablespoons heavy cream
½ teaspoon lemon juice
*   Salt to taste*

1. Crush the peppercorns and then cover the steaks on both sides with it. Melt the butter in a skillet and sauté the steaks for a few minutes on each side until medium rare. Remove the steaks from the skillet and set aside, keeping them in a warm oven.

2. Keep the skillet on the fire and add the cognac, Brown Sauce, and heavy cream. Cook the mixture on medium heat until it is reduced by a third of its original amount. Before pouring sauce over the steak add the lemon and salt.

SERVES 2

NOTE: Can be garnished with watercress.

Beef Bourguignon
BEEF BURGUNDY

2½ lbs. beef chuck, cut into 1½ in. cubes
½ cup salt pork, diced in ½-in. cubes
3 tablespoons vegetable oil
1½ tablespoons flour
2 cloves garlic, finely chopped
1 tablespoon chopped onions
1 oz. cognac
½ bottle Burgundy wine
2 cups beef broth
1 bouquet garni (bay leaf, thyme, parsley) tied in cheesecloth
Salt and freshly ground pepper to taste
16 small cooked onions
18 cooked mushroom caps
Chopped parsley

1. In a skillet sauté beef over a high flame with diced salt pork. Add oil. When meat is brown on all sides, add flour, garlic and onions. Let cook for 2 or 3 minutes.

2. Remove mixture to a kettle on top of stove. Pour cognac over it and flambé. when flame dies, add wine, beef broth, and bouquet garni. Cook, stirring, for 5 minutes. Cover.

3. Place in the oven at 375°F and bake for 1½ hours, until meat is tender. Add salt and freshly ground pepper to taste.

4. Garnish with onions, mushrooms, and parsley. Serve.

SERVES 6

NOTE: Can be served with small boiled potatoes.

Suprêmes de Volaille Cordon Bleu
CHICKEN BREASTS WITH HAM AND CHEESE

3 *whole chicken breasts*
  Salt and freshly ground pepper to taste
6 *thin slices prosciutto or other ham*
6 *paper-thin slices Swiss or Gruyère cheese*
  Flour for dredging
2 *eggs*
2 *teaspoons plus 2 tablespoons peanut, vegetable, or*
  corn oil
3 *cups fresh bread crumbs*
1 *cup grated Parmesan cheese*
6 *tablespoons butter*
  Brown chicken sauce (see page 67)

1. Have the chicken breasts split in half. Skin and bone them or have the butcher do it. Preferably and ideally the main wing bone should be left attached and it should be skinned but not boned. The main wing bone is not essential to preparing this dish, however.

2. Place the chicken breast halves skinned side down on a flat surface. Using a smooth-bottomed mallet or the bottom of a small heavy skillet, flatten each chicken breast in half. Try to avoid pounding holes in the flesh.

3. Sprinkle the breasts lightly with salt and pepper. Arrange one slice of prosciutto over the center of each breast half. Arrange a slice of cheese, doubled over, perhaps, on top of the ham. Fold the breast pieces over to enclose the ham and cheese. Pinch together around the edges.

4. Preheat the oven to 350° F.

5. Spoon the flour onto a flat surface.

6. Blend the eggs with 2 teaspoons of oil, salt, and pepper in a pie dish.

7. Blend the bread crumbs and Parmesan cheese in a dish such as a jelly roll pan.

8. Dip the filled chicken pieces first in flour, then in the beaten egg mixture, then roll in crumbs. Tap lightly with the flat side of a heavy kitchen knife to help the crumbs adhere.

9. Heat the butter and remaining 2 tablespoons of oil in 1 or 2 heavy skillets and brown the chicken pieces about 1 or 2 minutes to a side. Arrange the pieces in a baking dish and place in the oven. Bake about 5 to 6 minutes. Serve on hot plates and spoon a little brown chicken sauce around each serving.

SERVES 6

Filet of Sole Bonne Femme

5 tablespoons sweet butter
Salt and freshly ground white pepper to taste
¼ cup finely chopped shallots
1½ cups sliced mushrooms
1 tablespoon chopped fresh parsley
6 filets of sole
½ cup dry white wine
1 cup Fish Broth (see page 68)
1 tablespoon flour
1 cup heavy cream

1. Butter an au gratin dish with 1 tablespoon of butter. Sprinkle the dish with salt and pepper, the shallots, mushrooms, and parsley.

2. Place the filets of sole on top, and add the wine and 1 cup of fish broth. Bring to a boil. Now, cover and place in the oven at 400° F. for 5 to 6 minutes.

3. Meanwhile, mix 1 tablespoon of flour and 2 tablespoons of butter to a paste.

4. Remove the filets from the oven and arrange them on a platter.

5. Stir the butter and flour mixture into the juice in the au gratin dish and bring to a boil on top of the stove. Add the cream and reduce to the consistency of syrup and remove from the heat. Now add another 2 tablespoons of butter and mix into the sauce.

6. Correct the seasoning and pour over the sole. Put the platter into the broiler and glaze until golden brown.

SERVES 6

SAUCES

Fond Brun
BROWN SAUCE

3 lbs. veal bones chopped in 3- to 4-in. pieces
2 lbs. beef bones
1 large onion, coarsely chopped
1 cup coarsely chopped carrots
½ cup coarsely chopped celery
½ cup flour
½ teaspoon dried thyme
2 cloves garlic, coarsely chopped
Salt to taste
5–6 crushed peppercorns
1 large bay leaf
3 quarts water
3 chopped fresh tomatoes
1 cup tomato paste
½ cup parsley sprigs
5–6 mushrooms, chopped

1. Preheat oven to 400° F.

2. Combine the bones, onions, carrots, and celery in a large roasting pan. Place in the oven and bake for 30 minutes. Stir the mixture to prevent from browning too fast. Sprinkle with flour, and add the thyme, garlic, salt, peppercorns, and bay leaf. Bake gently for 15 minutes.

3. Transfer ingredients to a large kettle and add 1 quart of water to the roasting pan. Heat water over moderate heat, stirring to dissolve the brown particles that cling to the bottom and sides of the pan.

4. Add this to the kettle with the remaining water. Add the chopped tomatoes, tomato paste, parsley, and mushrooms, and bring to a boil, then simmer for 2 hours. Skim occasionally to remove foam and fat from the surface.

5. Strain the liquid and cool. This sauce can be stored in the refrigerator for a week or frozen for later use.

YIELDS 2 QUARTS

Fond Brun de Volaille
BROWN CHICKEN SAUCE

3 lbs. chicken wings, backs, and necks
¾ cup coarsely chopped onion
¾ cup coarsely chopped carrots
¾ cup coarsely chopped celery
6 sprigs parsley
½ teaspoon thyme
1 small bay leaf
2 tablespoons flour
2 cups fresh or canned chicken broth
  Salt and freshly ground pepper to taste
3 tablespoons Madeira wine
2 tablespoons butter

1. Cut the chicken pieces into 2-in. lengths, leaving the skin on but discarding any excess fat. Place the pieces in a heavy skillet and cook, without adding oil or other fat, about 30 minutes, stirring frequently. The chicken skin will give up its own fat. The pieces should be quite brown but do not burn.

2. Add the onion, carrots, celery, parsley, thyme, and bay leaf and cook uncovered about 30 minutes longer, stirring frequently.

3. Sprinkle with flour and stir. When the pieces are evenly coated, add the chicken broth, salt, and pepper to taste. Cook 20 minutes, stirring.

4. Pour the mixture into a food press or food mill, pressing the solids to extract as much liquid as possible. Discard the solids. There should be about 1⅓ to 1½ cups of sauce. Pour the sauce into a saucepan and add 2 tablespoons of wine. Simmer 5 minutes. Just before serving add the remaining wine and swirl in the butter.

YIELDS ABOUT 1½ CUPS.

Fumet de Poisson
FISH BROTH

    3 lbs. fish bones, including heads, gills removed
    3 tablespoons butter
    1 small onion sliced
    ⅓ cup chopped carrots
    ⅓ cup chopped celery
    ⅓ cup chopped leeks
2 or 3 sprigs of parsley
    2 tablespoons chopped shallots
    1 bay leaf
      Pinch of dried thyme
    1 teaspoon black peppercorns, crushed
    1 cup dry white wine
    4 cups water
      Salt to taste

1. Chop the bones and head into small pieces.

2. Heat the butter in a saucepan. Add fish bones and head. Cook 1 minute, stirring. Add onions, carrots, celery, leeks, parsley, sprigs, shallots, bay leaf, thyme, and peppercorns. Cook for 2 to 3 minutes.

3. Add the wine, water, and salt. Bring to a boil and let simmer for 15 to 20 minutes.

4. Strain the liquid through a fine china cap or fine sieve. Discard the solids.

YIELDS ABOUT 4½ CUPS

Velouté de Poisson
FISH VELOUTÉ

2 tablespoons butter
2 tablespoons flour
2 cups Fish Broth (see page 68)
½ cup chopped mushrooms
  Salt and white pepper to taste

1. Melt butter in a saucepan. Mixing with a wire whisk, add the flour. When blended, add the fish broth and mushrooms, stirring rapidly with the whisk until thickened and smooth. Let simmer gently for about 15 minutes.

2. Strain the sauce, add salt and white pepper to taste, and cool.

YIELDS 2 CUPS

NOTE: Can be stored in the refrigerator for 1 week.

Fumet de Truite
TROUT BROTH

Bones, skin and trimmings from 3 trout, including
  head and tail
1 cup dry white wine
1 cup water
3 sprigs fresh parsley
3 shallots, sliced
3 peppercorns
  Salt to taste
½ bay leaf

1. Combine all the ingredients in a saucepan. Bring to a boil and cook over relatively high heat for about 15 minutes.

2. Drain and discard solids.

YIELDS ABOUT 1¼ CUPS

Sauce Tomate à la Creme
TOMATO CREAM SAUCE

½ lb. ripe red tomatoes
2 tablespoons butter
1 tablespoon finely chopped onion
1 tablespoon thinly sliced shallots
  Salt and freshly ground pepper to taste
1¼ cups Trout Broth (see page 69)
1 cup heavy cream
Juice of ½ lemon

1. Core the tomatoes and cut into cubes. Set aside.

2. Heat 1 tablespoon of the butter and add the onion and shallots. Cook until wilted and add the tomatoes. Salt and pepper to taste. Cook briefly and add the trout broth. Reduce to about 1 cup.

3. Add the heavy cream and cook about 5 minutes.

4. Put the sauce through a fine sieve, preferably a French sieve known as a chinois. Put the sauce in a saucepan and add salt to taste, and lemon juice. Swirl in the remaining tablespoon of butter.

YIELDS ABOUT 2 CUPS

Celery Root Remoulade

1 lb. peeled celery root
  Juice of ½ lemon
1 cup mayonnaise
1 tablespoon Dijon mustard
1 tablespoon chopped sour pickles
½ tablespoon chopped capers
½ tablespoon chopped parsley
½ teaspoon chopped fresh tarragon
½ teaspoon chopped fresh chervil
  Salt and freshly ground black pepper to taste

1. Cut the celery root in quarters and then into julienne strips. Place the pieces in a salad bowl and squeeze the juice of half a lemon and mix.

2. In a separate bowl mix the remaining ingredients into the mayonnaise and season with salt and pepper to your taste.

3. Add the mayonnaise sauce to the celery root and mix gently. Keep refrigerated.

SERVES 6

Sauce Vinaigrette
FRENCH DRESSING

3 tablespoons wine vinegar
¾ tablespoons imported Dijon mustard
Salt and freshly ground pepper to taste
6 tablespoons vegetable oil
1 clove garlic, crushed (optional)
1 beaten egg yolk (optional)

1. In a mixing bowl put vinegar, mustard, salt, and pepper. Mix with a wire whisk. If you so prefer garlic and/or egg yolk, mix in as well.

2. Gradually add oil, stirring with wire whisk until blended. Chill dressing.

SERVES 4

NOTE: You can add chopped parsley, chopped chives, freshly chopped tarragon, and shallots.

DESSERTS

Crème Caramel

6 oz. sugar
½ quart milk
2 vanilla beans
3 whole eggs plus 4 yolks

1. Make caramel, by bringing to a boil in a small saucepan, using 2 oz. of sugar and a little water, until mixture turns a light shade of brown.

2. Divide the mixture evenly among 6 cups.

3. Boil the milk with the vanilla beans.

4. Blend the remaining 4 oz. of sugar with the eggs. Then mix with the boiling milk.

5. Fill the cups with the preparation and place in a baking dish. Fill baking dish half full of boiling water until it reaches half-way up the side of the cups. Bake at 375° F for 20 minutes.

SERVES 6

Crêpes Normandie

Batter:

1½ cups flour
4 eggs
1¾ cups milk
¼ lb. (1 stick) melted butter
Dash of salt
Dash of sugar

Mix all the ingredients together and make small crêpes on top of the stove, as in recipe on page 38).

Filling:

> 6 *Golden or Red Delicious apples*
> 2 *oz. (½ stick) butter*
> ⅓ *cup sugar*
> 2 *tablespoons Calvados*
>   *Confectioners sugar*

1. Peel, core, and dice the apples.

2. Sauté the apples with the butter and sugar until nicely browned. Let cool slightly and add the Calvados.

3. Fill the crêpes with the mixture, then fold. Arrange the crêpes on a platter, sprinkle with confectioners sugar, and glaze under the broiler.

SERVES 6

Chocolate Mousse Cake

Recipe of Raymond Richez

½ lb. Baker's German sweet chocolate, broken up
½ cup milk
¼ cup sugar
 3 egg yolks
½ lb. butter at room temperature
 1 cup heavy cream
 1 Genoise cake, bought or homemade
¼ cup white rum
 1 tablespoon confectioner's sugar
   Sabayon, flavored with rum (see page 126)

1. Use a double boiler or place a one-quart metal bowl over a saucepan into which it fits snugly. Put two inches water in saucepan so that bottom of bowl barely touches water. Place chocolate, milk, egg yolks and sugar in bowl and beat constantly with whisk until chocolate is melted.

2. Remove from heat and beat over water until mixture resembles a chocolate custard.

3. Lift bowl from water and set on cool surface. Beat until mixture is warm but not cold. Add butter and beat until mixture is smooth and reaches room temperature. Whip cream and fold into mixture.

4. Split Genoise and use to line sides and bottom of a 8½ × 4½ × 2½ in. pan. Reserve scraps. Sprinkle with rum. Fill pan with mousse mixture. Set extra mousse aside and chill cake overnight. Unmold cake on plate; frost with extra mousse. Make cake crumbs in food processor with Genoise scraps. Sprinkle over top and sides of cake. Press lightly to keep them in place. Sprinkle cake with confectioner's sugar. Chill until served.

5. Serve cake sliced on serving plates and top with Sabayon Sauce.

YIELD 6 TO 8 SERVINGS

Baked Apples

Recipe of Raymond Richez

16 Rome Beauty baking apples
16 tablespoons sugar
1 quart water
¼ lb. butter
1 lb. apricot preserves
1 cup brandy
Dab of whipped cream

1. Remove the core from each apple with a small apple corer. Remove a ring of the skin from the mid-section of each.

2. Place the apples in a large sauté pan (should hold 16 apples only), and pour 1 tablespoon of sugar into the middle of each apple, or enough to fill core.

3. Pour water into the pan containing the apples. Cut the butter stick into 16 squares and place one square on top of each apple.

4. Bring the liquid to a boil on top of the stove, then place on middle shelf of a 375° F oven and bake for 45 minutes or until apples are soft.

5. Remove the pan from the oven, and one at a time place apples in individual bowls. Return the pan with its juices to stove and stir in the apricot preserves. Bring to a boil, lower heat, and then simmer for about 15 minutes, or until liquid thickens and reduces to about 1 quart. Remove from heat.

6. Stir brandy into liquid and then pour over the apples, dividing evenly. Serve the apples warm and top with a dab of whipped cream.

SERVES 16

Twenty Americans whose performances in twenty
fields, from defense to decathlons, show the
X factor, the unknown-but-plus quantity that makes

CHAMPIONS

1. VICE-ADMIRAL HYMAN RICKOVER, a spare, weary-looking man, proceeds on one premise: "The more you sweat in peace the less you bleed in war." In that belief, he stubbornly pushed through the program to build the first atomic submarine, "Nautilus," guarded its progress with the irascible tenacity of a tern watching its eggs, swung away from its launching not to a rest but to an attack on American education: in brief, no meat, no guts, no future. Clearly not raised on Constructive Play, Rickover once said: "Nature seems to want to work for those who work hardest for themselves."

2. JEAN VERGNES, chief chef at the Colony Restaurant in New York, now commands the kitchen that once prompted Jimmy Walker (then Mayor of New York) to make the Colony more accessible to his black Rolls-Royce by changing the direction of traffic on its street. A naturalized American, Jean Vergnes trained in Grenoble, works now with intelligent energy, prefers talking to eating but not to cooking.

3. JEAN KERR is clearly prettier than, and thought by some to be funnier than, all the prime-time funnymen put together. Her gentle lure is Normality Bewildered; her tactic, gentle inquiry veering suddenly toward total devastation.

Never as bemused as she sounds in print, Mrs. Kerr—part of whose new book, *The Snake Has All the Lines*, appeared in Vogue—was described by Phyllis McGinley as a woman "who buttons her sweaters unevenly and forgets her lipstick, and her husband hasn't spoken a cross word to her in years."

4. FRED ASTAIRE danced his way from the Orpheum Circuit to become the lean, top-hatted, nonchalant charmer who danced over furniture in musicals of the Twenties, on ceilings in movies of the Thirties, the undepressed pleasure of the Depression years. Down from the ceiling and *On the Beach*, he never danced a step. Status now: best dancer, most durable looks. All based on bones: Very Good Bones.

From Vogue *Magazine, 1961*

IV

THE COLONY

As he had promised, Claudius called me into his office one day and introduced me to a gentleman by the name of Gene Cavallero. Gene told me he needed a new chef to start immediately at his restaurant and offered me the position. I asked him somewhat brazenly what kind of a place he owned. He replied, "I own The Colony." I then asked if he meant the Colony Club. At that point Claudius cut in and said, "No, Jean, Gene is the owner of The Colony *Restaurant,* on Sixty-first Street and Madison Avenue." It dawned on me then whom I was speaking with.

At this time in the 1950s The Colony Restaurant was one of the two most popular and prestigious dining establishments in New York City. (The other was Le Pavillon.) I was stunned. I told Gene that I was only twenty-nine-and-a-half years old. I explained that I was confident I could perform the job, but made it clear to him that I spoke very little English. He replied that at The Colony you didn't have to speak English. The crew was mostly French, with some Italians, and the menu was all in French.

It was very rare, at this time, for a person of my age to be considered for the position of executive chef of a *grand luxe* restaurant. Most men toiled in the kitchen until they were forty-five or fifty years old before becoming head chefs. But Claudius and Gene expressed such confidence in my abilities and experience that I said I would accept the job. As I left the meeting, my thoughts centered on the potential opportunities that lay ahead. I knew this was the chance of a lifetime. This was the culmination of all my prior training. I had worked at every station leading up to head chef and was now being given the opportunity to be in charge of the entire cuisine. I would now decide what the menu would be. I would be able to experiment and introduce new dishes. I would decide the seasonal meats, poultry, fish and vegetables that would be bought. All of this was very exciting to me.

My euphoria disappeared, however, when I arrived at The Colony on August 21, 1951, to begin work and realized what I'd gotten myself into. As Gene brought me into the kitchen and I looked at twenty-seven faces considerably older than my own—most of the men were in their forties and fifties—I asked myself, "What am I doing here?" It wasn't that I was afraid, but I was no fool either. I had worked in kitchens long enough to know that older chefs sometimes resented taking orders from men who'd spent less time learning the ropes. Would they accept me?

Gene introduced me to the crew and said, "This is Jean. He is going to be the new chef. Charlie is going to stay on for a couple of weeks to show him how the kitchen functions. Then you will follow Jean's lead." The expressions on the faces of the crew showed they were skeptical. Charlie was about sixty-six years old. He had been the executive chef for several years and was ready to retire. He was a great guy, a real pro, who took a liking to me right away when he realized what I knew and saw what I could do.

The first three weeks were tough ones, but eventually the crew came to realize that my abilities were legitimate. Instead of acting like the pompous chef, I made it a point to meet with each man. I scheduled my time so that I would work with each of them separately at his respective station. After watching how he did something, I would show him how I wanted it done if I did not approve of it. I was taught that there is only one way to do things right: no shortcuts. One thing that has always been a source of pride for me is the rapport I had with my crew at The Colony. Of the twenty-seven men who worked with me in the kitchen, only one left during the twelve years that I was the chef. And this individual left because he was caught stealing some merchandise from the restaurant. I will always remember the friendship I shared with my crew, especially with my two assistant chefs, Raymond Vaudard and Nicholas Kerdoncuff.

This is not to say that my transition to the post of executive chef was entirely smooth. One problem that needed to be remedied quickly concerned Gene's in-law, Mr. Rossett. In my first few weeks on the job I noticed that Mr. Rossett apparently had the responsibility of dealing with the food suppliers. At night, after the dinner service, this man would approach me and ask me what fish and meat and produce I would be needing the next day. I said to myself, "What's going on here?" It was understood in the trade that the executive chef is the man in charge when it comes to dealing with suppliers. After all, Gene expected the utmost in quality for a good price. If he received any criticism of either of these, I would be the one who got the flak for it. So I told Gene that I would prefer Rossett not be in the kitchen anymore. He apparently understood because the very next day Rossett was in charge of the wine inventory.

Regarding food suppliers, I remember that one day a man walked into the kitchen and said, in Italian-accented English, "Let me speak to the chef." I told him I was the chef. He introduced himself as Phil Rozzo, told me he was a fish supplier and asked me if I would be interested in his services. When I looked at this man I just had this feeling that he was like me, from the other side, and I trusted him. Though most of our conversation was carried on with hand signs—his English was as bad as mine—we managed to understand each other. A simple handshake meant we had a deal. Though I occasionally bought fish from other suppliers, Phil was to become my main supplier during my twelve years at The Colony. He built his company from a little business into one of the powerhouses at Fulton Fish Market, which is something that I and many of my confreres felt was a testament to his quality. Later I would do business with his son, Phil Jr., when I opened Le Cirque. The rapport between a chef and a supplier is a crucial one, because so much depends on a product's quality. Fish, especially, must be extra fresh or you can bet you will hear about it from both the customers and your boss.

For those who lack familiarity with The Colony Restaurant, it was a fashionable gathering place for America's high society in New

Rendering of The Colony's dining room.

York in the 1940s, '50s, and early '60s. The clientele included the Vanderbilts, Astors, Kennedys, Rockefellers, and many other celebrities, politicians, heads-of-state and society figures. It was "the place" for America's aristocracy to gather in a sophisticated fashion to wine and dine. I remember vividly those times when I would walk into a full dining room in the evening to say hello to some of the more important clients. Every gentleman, save none, had on a tuxedo, and every woman was wearing an elegant long gown. It was quite impressive.

Gene Cavallero, who owned The Colony along with Mr. Florentino, had built the restaurant into the kind of place it was through hard work and by making sure the establishment's clients were well catered to. Cavallero and Florentino, along with Henri Soulé of Le Pavillon, were the leaders of New York's gastronomic hierarchy at the time. They were old pros who taught me and many others valuable lessons in how to run a *grand luxe* restaurant.

I think that if there was one important difference between The Colony and Le Pavillon, it was probably the people each catered to. Le Pavillon, because of Henri Soulé's French background, attracted a more European clientele. Le Pavillon was much more French in its dining-room approach, too, than was The Colony. The people that frequented The Colony tended to be members of the American aristocracy, and the restaurant took many liberties with its dining-room decor, such as installing the blue-and-white-striped tent that became the hallmark of the barroom. As the story goes, in 1938 someone suggested to Gene that The Colony stay open during the summer season, instead of closing when the elegant people traveled to Europe. Hearing the idea, a decorator recommended that a tent be installed in the barroom. The tent has been there ever since. In fact, when I left The Colony, the tent was being replaced with a new one. I took the old tent and brought it home, where I used it to cover my firewood pile. It held much nostalgia. But these differences in the two restaurants were really cosmetic. Both places were hallmark dining institutions with classic French menus.

I came to regard Gene as my second father because of everything he taught me and because of the respect I came to have for him. He handled every problem and situation with consummate class, composure and professionalism. I owe more to Gene for the direction my life took—while with him and afterward—than any other person I know. Not only did he give me the opportunity to become executive chef of The Colony when I was not yet even thirty years old, but, once there, he helped me gain the crucial exposure I needed to make myself known to the public. He gave me the opportunity to perform numerous cooking demonstrations on radio, TV and at Gimbels and Bloomingdale's department stores. He made sure that I came out from the kitchen every night to say hello to the clients, to check to see how their dinners were, or perhaps to suggest one of the specials. He said to me, "Jean, remember to do like I do—no matter who you are talking with, whether there is a problem, whatever, always remember to keep smiling." He also told me something I will never forget. He said, "Jean, always remember, a good restauranteur must be deaf, blind and dumb. Deaf because you hear things that should not be heard, blind because you see things that you don't want to see and dumb because you have seen and heard things you cannot repeat." He was so right. Later, I would open Le Cirque restaurant with another member of The Colony, Sirio Maccioni. If it had not been for the public exposure Gene had provided, Sirio and I would never have been able to lure the clientele to Le Cirque that we ultimately did.

I have many rich memories of my years at The Colony. In culinary terms, it was probably the height of my creative abilities. I produced what I consider to be some of my best recipes during these years. The process of creating a recipe, like any art form, is a very personalized thing. When I want to create something new, I don't take out a pad and pen to write it down. On the contrary, I begin by picturing myself in the kitchen. I know where everything is: the spices here, the cream there, the meat here. I visualize all these ingredients and start to put them together in my mind. I actually make the entire recipe in my head and after satisfying myself with all the elements, I test the idea. Then it is just a matter of refining and adjusting the ingredients to provide the best, most pleasing taste.

This is exactly how I created such Colony specialties as Chicken Gismonda, Seafood Crepes and Clams Blinis. Also, the Tripe à la mode de Caen, for which I won the Grand Prix de France award in 1958, and the Lapin Diable à la Creme, which brought me the Grand

Conducting a cooking demonstration at Bloomingdale's department store.

Prix de l'America award in 1959. There is no greater satisfaction for me as a chef than to create a new recipe, place it in the public arena and watch the customers taste and enjoy it. A chef, like a painter, relies entirely on the public for his triumphs and failures. Luckily, I enjoyed many more of the former.

One of these early triumphs was my recipe for Clams Blinis. It was a very young Craig Claiborne, just beginning a career as food editor for The New York *Times*, who came to The Colony to dine and warmly received this dish. Later, my recipe for Seafood Crepes would be voted the most popular recipe of that year by the readership of his column. My Chicken Gismonda was yet another success, appealing to those who tended to be conscious of their weight.

Opera star Licia Albanese beams her pleasure as she is served by Chef Jean Vergne of the Colony Restaurant, who created and named special dish for the soprano.

Cooking Up a Dish for a Famed Diva

By PRUDENCE PENNY

OF ALL the media of entertainment, Grand Opera seems to leave the most lasting impression—at least when it comes to naming specially prepared dishes of food after its stars. The public has accepted "Chicken Tetrazzini," "Melba Toast," and "Peach Melba."

Latest to have a specialty named after her is Licia Albanese, the great soprano of the Metropolitan. Whipped up by Chef Jean Vergne of the Colony, it goes like this:

SUPREME OF TURKEY a la LICIA ALBANESE
Turkey, 12-15 lbs.
Butter
Mushrooms
Spinach
Truffles
Parmesan Cheese
Flour
Seasonings
Parsley

Boil turkey until it's about three-quarters done. Remove from pot, saving juices for gravy. When cold, slice off white meat from bones into "supremes" or individual servings. Rub pieces of meat with flour and with bread crumbs mixed with Parmesan cheese. Saute meat slowly in butter on both sides until lightly browned.

Arrange cooked spinach on long platter and place pieces of meat on spinach. Brown butter in frying pan and add finely sliced mushrooms and, at the last minute, truffles which have been blanched and sliced. Pour over supremes.

Before serving, surround supremes with gravy (made from juice). Garnish with finely chopped parsley and serve very hot. Should make four to six portions.

Chef's Favorite at the Colony

Chic Set Votes for Chicken

By LYN ZWAHL

For 40 years now, Gotham-ites and The Colony have carried on the most durable and scandal-less love affair ever witnessed in the shifting social scene.

This is not so amazing when you consider that The Colony, an elegant dining place at 30 E. 61st St., has been under the same leadership during the long romance. The name synonymous with the restaurant is Cavallero.

Gene Cavallero Sr. started at The Colony as headwaiter in 1919 and shortly after, with a partner, bought the place. Now his son, Gene Cavallero Jr., is carrying on with all his father's devotion to French haute cuisine.

Socialites, local and international, scramble for position noon and night, since a kind of tradition dictates that being seated at one of the front tables in the formal dining room depends on your rung in the social ladder.

Chef's Favorite Dish.

Nevertheless, the plushy atmosphere with its crystal chandeliers, cherry velvet seats and fresh flowers at each table daily (red roses or pink carnations) is only outdone by the acknowledged excellence of the food itself.

Presiding over the French kitchen is a friendly, handsome young chef, Jean Vergnes, who has been with The Colony for 10 years. The dish he chose to prepare for us, which he confided was a favorite with the ladies, is the Colony's Supreme de Volaille Gismonda, $3.75 on the menu. More simply, Breast of Chicken Gismonda.

An excellent idea for an "at home" luncheon party and certainly ample for dinner, it is an entree which is easily prepared, at least by the well-coordinated hands of Chef Vergnes.

In preparation for just one serving, Mr. Vergnes took one

As served at the Colony and a favorite with the ladies at lunch, Supreme de Volaille Gismonda; delicately tender breast of chicken over spinach and topped with thinly sliced sauteed mushrooms.

lightly to a thickness between ⅛ to ¼-inch.

Use High Heat.

Both sides of the breast are salted and peppered lightly and dipped in flour. Then it is dipped into a bowl containing one beaten egg and from there into a mixture of bread crumbs and Parmesan cheese (⅔ breadcrumbs and ⅓ cheese). It is important that the meat be well coated with this mixture. (To insure this, take an ordinary knife and make crisscrosses on each side of the breast.)

Next, place a skillet over very high heat. Melt about a tablespoon of butter and when it is slightly brown place the

a little longer on a home range (four or five minutes on each side) since the heat intensity is not so great as on a restaurant range.

While the breast of chicken is cooking—or, if it's more practical, prepare this before you start the chicken—cook a desired amount of spinach in one pan and saute some sliced mushrooms in another. Keep warm.

Then, when the chicken is cooked to a golden turn, place the spinach in the center of a plate and the breast of chicken on it. Top with the sliced mushrooms, an additional teaspoon of hot melted butter over the top, and garnish with parsley. The Col

Jean Vergnes, the Colony's chef, dips the skinned and boned breast of chicken into one beaten egg during the preparation.

Two articles that appeared about my recipes.

My years at The Colony were full of experimentation with new dishes that I felt might "catch on" with people who ate there. This, by the way, is one of the subtle powers of a chef, of which not everyone is aware: a chef can create a demand for a food product simply by introducing it to his diners in an imaginative way. Like a piece of music, which is actually a reshuffling of notes that have always existed and have been used before, a recipe is a recombination of ingredients that are familiar to everyone. It is this chance to recombine, to exercise a creative free hand, that makes the job of a chef exciting and rewarding. The chef's profession is difficult in terms of the hours one must put in and the demands it places on one's skill and imagination; but for someone of my temperament, there is no other profession.

My recipes intimate and reflect my classic French background. In matters of preparation I am a disciple of Auguste Escoffier, and I closely follow his classical recipes. The Escoffier cuisine, like every work of art, is constantly open to new interpretation. For example, when I was an apprentice we were taught that the only foods to garnish with were truffles, tomatoes, leeks and hard-boiled eggs. But when I started to garnish my dishes at The Colony, I used any garnish that was edible and added to the overall appearance of the dish, such as carrots, zucchini and so on. Alterations must also occasionally be made because of the seasonality of fresh food supplies. Oftentimes, I would vary something to better suit the eating habits of The Colony's clientele. In fact, even today I can vividly recall what some of the better-known clientele used to order. If Salvador Dali was eating dinner he would ask me, without fail, for a Grand Marnier Soufflé. The late Duchess of Windsor would always want a salad of crabmeat or a minute steak. When I came out to the dining room to say hello to Frank Sinatra, he would ask me to prepare a coté de veau milanaise—very dry. Elizabeth Taylor liked to have mussels mariniere. And Charles Revson always ordered coté de veau grilled—no salt, no butter. As a chef, you must be able and willing to satisfy the customers' oftentimes fickle tastes.

Those who frequented The Colony were, for the most part, sophisticated and experienced gourmets. They appreciated good service and fine cuisine and liked to dine in comfort, but they also liked a show. This "show" that I speak of was the personality of the dining room as it manifested itself in the quality of food served, the flair of the waiters and the delight of the customers. With its high ceilings and red-and-white decor, the personality of The Colony was one of constant gaiety and conviviality. From the first taste of soup to the lighting of the last flambé, the kitchen staff and the management worked together to keep it this way.

There were, however, those times when mistakes were made. One particular incident that comes to mind still causes me to chuckle. It was an evening when Mr. and Mrs. William Kissam Vanderbilt, along with two other couples, came to The Colony for dinner. They had ordered pheasant, and the maître'd came out with the dish and displayed it to the party. He proceeded to place the pheasants on the table and began carving. Well, for one reason or another, the maître'd caused the bird to slip, and the entire pheasant, along with a full glass of wine, fell onto the members of the party, and then onto the floor. Quickly, Gene came over to the Vanderbilts and began apologizing for what had just happened. The Vanderbilts happened to be very good customers, as well as friends to Gene, and so all was quickly forgotten.

However, the pheasants, which now had to be changed, would take more than forty-five minutes to prepare, and the party indicated that they did not have enough time to wait. So Gene called me to the table and explained the situation. He gave me a wink, and I picked up his cue right away. I told the party not to worry, that I had some pheasants in the oven for another party, but because they were eating so slowly we could substitute them. The truth of the matter was, we brought their fallen pheasants back into the kitchen, cleaned them up, reheated them a few minutes and then served them for the second time.

One waiter who was infamous for the mistakes he would make was a fellow by the name of Angelo. He brought more laughs to the crew than all of us combined. Before I describe one common blunder of his, it must be understood that the dining room was set up in such a way that the waiter could grab whatever sauce was needed for a particular dish. Both the Sabayon Sauce, made for desserts, and the Hollandaise Sauce, for appetizers and entrées, are yellowish in color. Well, this son-of-a-gun Angelo was always rushing, and more often than not he would end up serving the Sabayon with asparagus and

At The Colony with Gene Cavallero (center) and chef Nicolas Kerdoncuff (left).

the Hollandaise sauce with beignet soufflés. What became even funnier is that some of the customers would unwittingly compliment me on the choice of sauce I had served. At times it seemed that the better the compliment, the more sure I was that Angelo had given them the wrong sauce.

Another time, Angelo served a turkey that I had prepared, usually served with a brown sauce. Well, once again Angelo was so hurried that instead of serving the brown sauce, he mistakenly served a chocolate sauce. Ironically, the customers, who were Mexican, asked me for the recipe. I did not know at the time that such a dish actually existed. Yet, the gentleman told me that turkey with chocolate sauce was very popular in Mexico. In fact, he found my sauce to be the best he'd ever had. I have only Angelo to thank for helping to create this recipe, one born out of sheer accident.

I don't regret a minute of the twelve years I served as the executive chef at The Colony. Though the days were often long and the work hard, it was, as I've said, a period of my life in which I experienced great culinary development and critical recognition. As the executive chef it was my job to make up the menu each day and to decide what specials I would offer. Oftentimes my decision was based on the time of year, since Gene always wanted me to make sure we offered seasonal food specials. For example, if it was spring, I'd better have soft-shell crabs, baby lamb and asparagus on the menu. If it was winter or late fall, it would have to be rabbit, pheasant and venison. The menu would change with the season.

After Mr. Rossett was placed in charge of the wine inventory, it became my responsibility to do all the buying of the fish, meat and produce. I remember how I used to go two or three times a week to the Fulton Fish Market, and to Fourteenth Street to the butcher. All the buying was done after dinner. I would go down to Fulton about two or three o'clock in the morning and tell the fish vendor what I wanted and how much. It was the fish vendor's responsibility to deliver the fish to The Colony in the morning. I would then walk over to the butcher on Fourteenth Street, where I would select the cuts of veal, beef and lamb that I wanted and determine when the cuts would be marked for The Colony and delivered. One may ask how much sleep I was able to fit in with such a busy schedule. The answer is, very little, for after this buying I would usually take a bus

Chatting with vendors at Knickerbocker Meat Market, 1958. My good friend Raymond Richez, then chef at the Delmonico, is standing directly behind me.

up to Harlem and go dancing and listen to jazz. It was great to be young and full of energy, and in those days I never missed an opportunity to take advantage of it.

In my capacity as executive chef it was also my responsibility to call out each and every order the waiters brought into the kitchen. I was in charge of supervising the flow of orders coming in and making sure they went out properly to the right tables. Occasionally, I would go behind the range to prepare a dish for a customer, or if I wanted to try something new. But for the most part, the cooking was being done by Raymond and Nicolas, two very capable chefs whom I trusted implicitly.

The Colony was a major stepping-stone in my career, and I have Gene to thank for allowing me so many opportunities at such a young

age. He gave me carte blanche in running the kitchen and never
once questioned my buying. He demanded only that the food be of
the highest caliber.

I never thought the day would come when I would leave The
Colony, but it did. In 1962, Gene was ready to retire. He asked me
if I wanted to become a partner in the ownership of The Colony with
his son, Gene Cavallero Jr. With regret I told him that I couldn't
accept his kind offer. I explained that I would find it too difficult to
work with his son. Gene Jr. was receiving everything his father had
built, yet it seemed to me that he had very little appreciation for the
tireless commitment and attention to detail that had gone into it. I
just couldn't see the two of us forming an effective partnership.
Although my decision meant that I was passing up the chance to be
an owner, in hindsight I think it was a wise choice, since, a few
years after Gene retired, The Colony closed.

Before I left on June 11, 1962, Gene held a bittersweet farewell
dinner party for me. There were many watery eyes that night, mine
included. But I was leaving The Colony to pursue a rather interesting
job prospect, so my sadness was somewhat mitigated. I had received
many offers, even one that would have brought me back to France,
but I realized America was now my home, and here I would stay.
Following in the footsteps of my close friend Pierre Franey, who was
the chef of Le Pavillon while I was at The Colony and had recently
joined Howard Johnson's restaurant chain, I had accepted a position
as executive chef of the Stop & Shop chain in Boston.

I was recently in New York, walking along Sixty-first Street near
Madison, when I spotted the site where The Colony had once stood.
The building I remembered was no longer there. The entire façade
had been completely eliminated. The city planners, in their wisdom,
had torn it down to make way for co-ops. I stood in the street for
some time, staring at what was no longer there. It was at this point
that I fully realized that a whole era of lifestyle and dining was gone
forever. The *grand luxe* restaurants were no longer. I thought about
all the limousines that had driven up this street to drop off a movie
star, or a president, or a duke and duchess, at the steps of The
Colony. I thought about the brigade of twenty-seven men who worked
with me in the kitchen. And I realized that probably never again

would there be a restaurant that could claim equivalent celebrity status and gourmet haute cuisine.

The Colony was the place to be for more than four decades. It was a superior and unparalleled dining institution at which many a political and business decision was made while eating fois gras and sipping champagne. And though the physical structure is gone, for restaurateurs like myself The Colony's legend and spirit will live on.

APPETIZERS

Bisque de Homard
LOBSTER BISQUE

2 3–3½-lb. live lobsters
2¼ cups dry white wine
¾ cup flour
¾ cup butter
2 tablespoons vegetable oil
¼ cup plus 1 tablespoon cognac
¾ cup chopped onions
½ cup chopped carrots
⅓ cup chopped leeks (only the white part)
2 cups chopped fresh tomatoes
½ cup tomato paste
¼ teaspoon thyme
1 tablespoon fresh tarragon (or 1 teaspoon dried tarragon)
4 cups Fish Broth (see page 68)
Salt and freshly ground pepper to taste
2 cups heavy cream
1 cup milk

1. With a large knife cut the legs, claws, and tail off the lobster. Cut each part into 3 or 4 pieces. Separate the front of the lobster in half lengthwise. Take out the coral, tomally, and liquid, and reserve.

2. Add ¼ cup white wine and ¾ cup butter to the coral and tomally mixture. Mix it all up with a wire whisk to make a paste, which will be used to thicken the soup.

3. Place oil in a large skillet and when hot place the lobster pieces in, cook for 4 to 5 minutes, stirring pieces until they turn red. Add ¼ cup of cognac and ignite, then add onions, carrots, leeks, tomatoes, tomato paste, thyme, tarragon, 2 cups white wine, and the fish stock. Season with salt and pepper and add the mixture to the lobster parts. Mix all very well.

4. Cover the soup and simmer for 15 to 20 minutes. With a skimmer remove the lobster pieces and place on the side on a plate. When cool enough, remove the meat from the shells and set aside. Discard the shells and then coarsely chop the pieces of lobster breast with a cleaver. Add this to a pan and cook for 10 minutes, then strain through a sieve, pushing with a ladle to extract as much liquid as possible.

5. Add the cream and milk to the pot and bring to a boil. Season to taste if needed, stir in the tablespoon of cognac at the last minute with the diced lobster meat. Serve very hot.

SERVES 8

Bouillabaise

½ lb. boneless striped bass, cut in 1½-in. squares (or
        sea bass)
½ lb. boneless red snapper
½ lb. boneless monkfish
½ lb. boneless flounder
 6 large shrimp, shelled and deveined
 1 2-lb. lobster cut in quarters (6 pieces)
 2 teaspoons saffron
 1 tablespoon chopped garlic
½ cup chopped fresh fennel (or ¼ teaspoon fennel
        seeds)
 1 tablespoon chopped leeks
¼ cup chopped celery
 1 tablespoon chopped onions
 6 cups fish broth (see page 68)
 1 cup dry white wine
 1 tablespoon tomato paste
⅓ cup olive oil
   Pinch of cayenne pepper
   Pinch of dried thyme
 1 small bay leaf
   Salt to taste
18 mussels, well scrubbed
 6 littleneck clams
 2 cups chopped fresh tomatoes
 1 tablespoon chopped parsley
 1 tablespoon Pernod
12 croutons toasted and rubbed with fresh garlic (use
        French bread)

1. The night before marinate the following ingredients with 1
teaspoon of saffron: striped bass, red snapper, monkfish, flounder,
shrimp, and lobster.

2. Heat olive oil in a large, saucepan and add the garlic, fennel,
leeks, celery, and onions. Sauté these ingredients for a few minutes.

3. Now add the fish broth, white wine, tomato paste, remaining saffron, cayenne, thyme, bay leaf, and salt, and let simmer slowly for 10 minutes.

4. Add the marinated fish, cover the pot, and simmer for another 2 minutes. Then add the mussels, clams, chopped tomatoes, and parsley. Simmer for 5 minutes, covered. At the last minute add the Pernod.

5. Serve hot in soup bowls with 2 croutons on top, and some Rouille (see page 124).

SERVES 6 TO 8

Fish Chowder

3 lbs. haddock or cod, cleaned with head and tail
   removed (but reserved), body cut into 3-inch-
   thick steaks
2 cups water
   Salt and freshly ground black pepper to taste
   Pinch of dried thyme
½ bayleaf
¼ lb. lean salt pork with rind removed, diced into
   ¼-in. pieces
2 tablespoons butter
½ cup coarsely chopped onion
¼ cup finely chopped leeks
2 medium potatoes, peeled and finely diced
1 quart milk
1 cup heavy or light cream
2 drops Tabasco

1. Place the haddock or cod steak, head, and tail in a stainless steel casserole with water, salt, pepper, thyme, and bay leaf. Cook for about 15 minutes, and strain the broth. Cut the steak into 1-in. pieces and set both the stock and steak pieces aside.

2. In a 4-quart stainless-steel casserole, sauté the salt pork in 1 tablespoon of butter over moderate heat until crisp. Stir frequently with a wooden spoon. Add the onions and leeks, and cook until they are soft. Add the reserved broth and the potatoes, and cook for another 10 minutes until done.

3. Add the milk, cream, and fish meat. Let chowder simmer for 2 minutes. Before serving, add the remaining 1 tablespoon of butter and 2 drops of Tabasco.

SERVES 6

Mousse of Scallops

1 lb. bay scallops (sea scallops should be diced, if used)
Salt to taste
Pinch of cayenne pepper
Pinch of fresh grated nutmeg
2 whole eggs
2 cups heavy cream
Butter for greasing mold

1. Preheat oven to 375° F.

2. Put scallops into a food processor. Add salt, cayenne pepper, and nutmeg. Process for about 30 seconds. Gradually add the eggs and 1 cup of the heavy cream and continue mixing until thoroughly blended. Spoon the mixture into a mixing bowl.

3. Beat the remaining heavy cream until very firm, and fold it into the scallop mixture.

4. Butter the inside of a 4-cup soufflé mold. Scrape the scallop mixture into it. Smooth the top with a spatula and cover with buttered aluminum foil.

5. Set the mold in a basin of water on top of the stove, and bring to a boil.

6. Remove from the heat and place in the oven. Bake for 25 to 30 minutes.

7. Remove the aluminum paper, and unmold onto a round serving dish. Pour off or wipe away any liquid that may flow out. Serve with Beurre Blanc (see page 33) or Lobster Sauce (see page 222).

SERVES 4

NOTE: This recipe can be prepared the same way with sole, flounder, striped bass, or monkfish.

Mousse de Sole au Vin Blanc
MOUSSE OF SOLE WITH WHITE WINE SAUCE

> *butter for greasing the mold, a four cup souffle dish*
> 1-½ *lbs. boneless filet of sole (cut in 2-in. cubes)*
> *Salt and freshly ground white pepper to taste*
> *Pinch of ground nutmeg*
> *Pinch of cayenne pepper*
> 2 *cups heavy cream*
> 2 *whole eggs*
> 1 *tablespoon chopped black truffles*
> 2 *cups White Wine Sauce (see page 35)*

1. Preheat oven to 375° F.

2. Butter the mold. Keep it chilled.

3. Place the fish in a food processor with salt, pepper, nutmeg, and cayenne and process 30 seconds until you have a very smooth consistency.

4. Beat 1 cup of heavy cream until firm, and gently fold this into the sole purée.

5. Scrape the fish mixture into the mold and smooth the top with a spatula. Cover the top with aluminum foil.

6. Place the mold in a roasting pan full of boiling water, and place in the preheated oven for about 45 minutes.

7. Pour off any liquid that may have accumulated in the mold. Unmold the mousse onto a round serving dish and serve with White Wine Sauce.

SERVES 6 TO 8

NOTE: You can add 3 tablespoons of Hollandaise Sauce to the White Wine Sauce for a richer taste.

Mousse de Truite
TROUT MOUSSE WITH TOMATO CREAM SAUCE

*3 skinless, boneless trout filets, about ¾ lb. (reserve
        the bones to make a fish stock for a sauce)
    Salt and freshly ground pepper to taste
    Nutmeg to taste
2 cups heavy cream
3 large egg yolks
3 large whole eggs
    Tomato Cream Sauce (see page 70)*

1. Preheat the oven to 350° F.

2. Cut the filets into cubes and add them to the container of a food processor. Blend with salt, pepper, and nutmeg until finely chopped.

3. Gradually add the cream, egg yolks, and whole eggs. Blend to a fine pureé.

4. Generously butter a 5-cup charlotte mold and line the bottom with a round of buttered wax paper and spoon in trout mixture. Tap it down to pack compactly in the mold. Smooth the top over and cover with a round of wax paper.

5. Place the mold in a basin of water and bring the water to a boil on top of the stove. Place in the oven and bake 1 hour (see note).

6. Remove the mold and wipe off the bottom. Run a knife around the rim. Unmold onto a round platter. Serve with hot Tomato Cream Sauce.

SERVES 8

NOTE: 5-cup ring mold may be used. In that case this should be baked 30 minutes.

Gravlax
MARINATED SALMON

3–3½ lbs. fresh salmon
1 bunch very fresh dill (about 10 to 12 branches)
¼ cup coarse or kosher salt
¼ cup sugar
2 tablespoons crushed black peppercorns

1. The salmon should be cleaned and scaled, cut lengthwise, backbone and all small bones removed, and the skin should be left on. Place half of the salmon, skin down, in a glass or enamel casserole or baking dish. Wash the dill, shake dry, and remove any coarse lower stems. Chop coarsely.

2. In a bowl, combine the salt, sugar, and crushed peppercorns. Put half the dill on top of the salmon half, then sprinkle the salt mixture evenly over it. Top with the other half, sandwich fashion, skin side up. As the two pieces of fish will probably not be the uniform thickness, position them so one thick side is on top of one thin side.

3. Cover the fish with aluminum foil and on top of this place a rectangular plate, tray, plank—something that will exert even pressure on the fish and is a little larger in size. Weight down with a couple of heavy cans.

4. Keep refrigerated for at least 48 hours, up to three days total. While marinating, turn the fish every 12 hours, basting it with the liquid that accumulates, separating the halves to baste the inside of the salmon. Replace heavy cans and weights each time.

5. To serve, remove the fish from the marinade, scrape off the seasonings and dill, and pat dry. Place the separate halves, skin side down, on a carving board and slice thinly with a sharp knife. Cut slightly on the diagonal, holding the knife almost horizontal. Carefully detach the slices from the skin. Garnish with lemon wedges.

SERVES 10 TO 12

NOTE: Serve this dish with Sour Cream Dill Sauce with Mustard (see page 224), thin slices of buttered dark bread or toast, and Cucumber Salad (see page 162).

Soufflé au Roquefort
ROQUEFORT CHEESE SOUFFLE

6 tablespoons butter, plus butter to grease the molds
6 tablespoons flour
3 cups milk
1 tablespoon cornstarch
2 tablespoons water
½ lb. Roquefort cheese
10 eggs, separated
Freshly ground pepper to taste
Wax paper

1. Rub the inside of six 3-cup individual soufflé molds with butter and chill them well.

2. Melt the 6 tablespoons of butter in a saucepan and add the flour, stirring with a wire whisk until blended. Add the milk, stirring rapidly with the whisk until the mixture is thickened and smooth. Do not add salt; the cheese is salty. Simmer, stirring frequently, about 5 minutes. Blend the cornstarch with the water and add it, stirring rapidly. Cook about 2 minutes, stirring. Crumble or cube the Roquefort and add it, stirring until thoroughly blended and smooth.

3. Turn off the heat. Beat the yolks and add them, with the pepper, to the sauce. Cook, stirring vigorously, about 1 minute, and remove from the heat. Immediately scrape the sauce into a large mixing bowl. Butter a round of wax paper and place it, buttered side down, over the sauce. Let the sauce cool thoroughly.

4. Preheat the oven to 400° F.

5. Beat the whites until stiff. Add about a third of them to the sauce and fold them gently in. Add the remaining whites and fold them in with a rubber spatula. Spoon equal parts of the mixture into the chilled soufflé molds. Place the molds in a pan large enough to hold them. Place them in the oven and bake 15 minutes.

SERVES 6

Soufflé d'Epinard
SPINACH SOUFFLÉ

1 lb. spinach, chopped
4 oz. butter
2 oz. flour
1 pint milk
  Salt to taste
  Pinch of nutmeg
6 eggs, separated
¾ cup grated Parmesan cheese

1. Cook spinach in salted water, strain well, squeeze water out completely and chop finely.

2. Melt 3 oz. of the butter, add flour, mix well, add boiling milk and whip with a wire whisk, add salt and nutmeg and whip until boiling point. Remove from heat, add egg yolks, whipping fast, and the chopped spinach and cheese.

3. Whip the egg whites until very stiff and fold into the mixture.

4. Rub the inside of a soufflé mold with 1 oz. of butter. Fill the mold up to the top and cook for 35 minutes in a 350° F. oven. Serve immediately.

SERVES 6

Salade Gourmande
FOIE GRAS SALAD

Salad:

>½ lb. green beans, the fresher and smaller the better
>Salt
>
>24 asparagus
>Lettuce leaves, preferably from red leaf or Boston lettuce, although other Lettuce such as endive or watercress could be used
>1 large or 2 small black truffles, sliced and cut into fine (julienne) strips
>1 8-oz. can of pure foie gras

Dressing:

>1 teaspoon imported prepared mustard, preferably Dijon or Dusseldorf (do not use the baseball lot variety)
>Salt and freshly ground pepper to taste
>2 tablespoons cider vinegar
>¼ cup peanut oil
>¼ cup olive oil
>⅛ teaspoon sugar

1. Snip off and discard the tips of the green beans. Cut the beans into uniform 2-in. lengths. Drop the pieces into boiling salted water to cover and cook 5 to 8 minutes, depending on size. Do not overcook. When done, the pieces should be crisp-tender. Drain and let cool to room temperature.

2. Cut the tips, about 2 inches in length, from the asparagus. Set the remaining sections of the asparagus aside for another use such as in soups, salads, and so on. Rinse the asparagus tips well under cold running water. Drain and drop them into boiling salted water to cover. Cook 3 to 7 minutes, depending on thickness. When done, the pieces should be crisp-tender. Drain and let cool to room temperature.

3. When ready to serve, arrange a few lettuce leaves on 6 chilled individual salad plates. If red leaf lettuce is available, arrange it so that the red perimeter of the lettuce will show as a border for the salads.

4. Arrange equal portions of the green beans in the center of each salad, then a layer of asparagus tips. Sprinkle each serving with the shredded truffles. If the foie gras comes in a terrine or crock, spoon equal amounts of it in the center of the salads. If it is a "bloc" or tunnel-shape of foie gras, cut it into 12 portions. Arrange equal amounts of foie gras on each salad.

5. Place the mustard in a mixing bowl and add salt and pepper. Add the vinegar, stirring with a wire whisk. Gradually add the oils, stirring rapidly with the whisk. Add the sugar and blend. Spoon the sauce over the salads and serve, preferably with buttered toast or French bread.

SERVES 6

ENTRÉES

Clams with Blinis

36 littleneck clams
2 tablespoons finely chopped shallots
½ cup dry white wine
   Freshly ground black pepper
3 tablespoons butter
3 tablespoons flour
2 tablespoons Pernod, Ricard or other anise-flavored
   liquor
2 egg yolks
3 tablespoons heavy cream
4 teaspoons finely chopped parsley
1 tablespoon finely chopped tarragon
   A few drops of Tabasco sauce
18 Buckwheat Blinis (see page 105)

1. Open the clams or have them opened. Save the clams and liquid in separate batches. There should be about 1¼ cups clams and 1⅓ cups clam liquid. Chop the clams and set aside. Do not chop the clams too fine.

2. Add the chopped shallots and wine to a small skillet and cook down until almost but not all the wine has evaporated. Add the clam liquid. Add a generous amount of black pepper and bring to the boil.

3. Blend the butter and flour until smooth.

4. Remove the saucepan from the heat and gradually add the butter-flour mixture, a little at a time, stirring constantly with a wire whisk. When thickened, add 1 tablespoon of the Pernod and return to the heat.

5. Blend the yolks and cream and add gradually to the sauce, stirring constantly. Do not boil or the eggs will curdle. You must heat it, however, so that the yolks lose their raw taste.

6. Add the parsley and tarragon. Add Tabasco, remaining Pernod, and black pepper to taste.

7. Add the clams and heat without boiling. The more the clams cook the more they toughen.

8. Serve 3 blinis on each of 6 plates and spoon equal portions of the clams in sauce over.

SERVES 6

NOTE: The above recipe specifies, for a very good reason, the use of littleneck clams. When purchasing the clams, select the smallest ones available. The smallest clams are much more tender than, say, the larger cherrystones. Chowder clams would not be acceptable.

Buckwheat Blinis

2 teaspoons granular yeast
2 tablespoons plus ½ cup water
1 cup buckwheat flour, available in specialty food
    shops and health food stores
1 egg, lightly beaten
½ cup milk
2 tablespoons melted butter
    Salt to taste

1. To prepare the blinis, combine the yeast and 2 tablespoons water in a small bowl and stir to dissolve the yeast. Put the bowl in a warm place. Let stand about 5 minutes.

2. Put the flour in a mixing bowl and add the egg. Stir. Add the milk and remaining water, stirring constantly with a wire whisk. Add the melted butter and salt to taste and stir in the yeast mixture. Cover. Let stand in a warm place about 1 hour.

3. Heat a blini or crêpe pan. Rub lightly with butter. Spoon about 2 tablespoons of the blini batter into the pan and cook briefly until lightly browned and set on the bottom. Carefully turn with a spatula and cook until set and cooked through. Spoon onto a dish. Continue using the batter until all of it is used.

YIELDS ABOUT 18 BLINIS

Seafood Crêpes

16 Crêpes with Fine Herbes (see page 107)
1½ cups (approximately) Curry Sauce (see page 122)
1½ cups Sauce Piquante (see page 122)
3 tablespoons butter
2 tablespoons finely chopped shallots
⅓ cup dry white wine
1 tablespoon each finely chopped chives, parsley, and
      tarragon
1 cup finely diced lobster meat
1 cup finely diced shrimp
1 cup lump crabmeat
   Salt and freshly ground pepper
   Butter for brushing crêpes

1. Prepare the crêpes.

2. Start sauces. While they are simmering, prepare the filling.

3. Place the 3 tablespoons of butter in a saucepan and add the shallots. Cook briefly, stirring, and add the wine. Cook to reduce by half. Add the herbs and sea food and stir to blend. Sprinkle with salt and pepper to taste and cook briefly, stirring, until heated through.

4. Preheat the oven to warm.

5. Spoon equal portions of the mixture into the center of each crêpe and roll. Arrange the crêpes on a platter and brush with melted butter. Butter a sheet of wax paper nd place it buttered side down over the crêpes. Cover and place in the oven. Bake briefly, just until heated through—but not until piping hot.

6. Serve on hot plates, spooning a little of the Curry Sauce on half of each crepe, a little of the Sauce Piquante on the other half.

SERVES 8 TO 10

Crêpes with Fine Herbes

1½ cups sifted all-purpose flour
2 eggs
¼ teaspoon salt
2½ cups milk
1 tablespoon each chopped fresh tarragon, parsley,
*   and chives*
3 tablespoons melted butter

1. Combine the flour, eggs, and salt in a mixing bowl. Gradually add the milk, stirring constantly with a wire whisk.

2. Strain the batter into a mixing bowl, then add the herbs and melted butter.

3. Heat a 6-to-7-in. seasoned crêpe pan and brush it lightly with butter. Ladle a little of the batter in, swirling the pan around until the bottom is thoroughly covered with a thin coating. Cook until lightly browned on one side. Flip and cook briefly on the other side. The crêpe should not be brown on the second side. Repeat the procedure until the batter is used up.

YIELDS ABOUT 20 CRÊPES

Canapé d'Homard
LOBSTER CANAPÉ

3 1¼-lb. live lobsters
8 tablespoons butter, approximately
1 tablespoon chopped onion
1 tablespoon finely chopped shallots
¼ cup dry white wine
1 tablespoon white vinegar
1½ cups Brown Sauce (see page 66)
1 teaspoon dry mustard
2–3 tablespoons A-1 sauce
    Salt and freshly ground pepper to taste
¼ cup heavy cream
1 tablespoons chopped fresh tarragon
8 slices thin bread
¼ cup dry Sherry
¼ cup finely chopped parsley

1. Drop the lobsters into boiling salted water and cover. Boil 15 minutes and drain. Let cool.

2. In a saucepan, heat 1 tablespoon butter and add the onion and shallots. When wilted, add the wine and vinegar. Cook until almost completely reduced. Add the Brown Sauce, dry mustard, A-1 sauce, Tabasco, salt, and pepper. Simmer about 15 minutes and add the cream and 1 tablespoon chopped tarragon. Simmer 15 minutes longer.

3. Meanwhile preheat the oven to 350°F.

4. Cut the bread into 3-in. rounds and arrange them on a baking sheet. Brush with butter and bake, watching closely, until they are golden brown.

5. Meanwhile, remove the meat from the claws and tail of the lobsters. Cut the tail and claw meat into rounds or pieces about ¼ in. thick. Combine with the remaining lobster meat.

6. Heat 2 tablespoons of butter in a skillet and add the Sherry. Add the lobster and cook briefly just to heat through. Do not overcook or the meat will toughen.

7. Bring the sauce to the boil and add more chopped tarragon if the flavor is not strong enough. Swirl in 2 tablespoons of butter.

8. Arrange one piece of toast on each of 8 hot plates and add equal amounts of lobster to each piece of toast. Spoon the sauce over and sprinkle each serving with parsley.

SERVES 6 TO 8

Supreme de Volaille Gismonda
BREAST OF CHICKEN WITH MUSHROOMS AND SPINACH

4 chicken breasts, boned
Salt and white pepper to taste
Flour for dredging
1 egg
1 tablespoon water
¼ cup grated Parmesan cheese
¾ cup white bread crumbs
3 tablespoons butter
1 lb. cooked spinach
½ lb. mushrooms, sliced
2 tablespoons Brown Sauce (see page 66)
Chopped fresh parsley

1. Remove skin from chicken breasts and pound meat (rolling pin may be used). Season with salt and pepper and dredge with flour. Dip meat in egg which has been lightly beaten with water. Bread with the mixture of cheese and crumbs.

2. Heat 2 tablespoons butter in skillet and brown meat on both sides, about 10 minutes on each side.

3. Make a bed of coarsely chopped spinach on serving platter, arrange chicken breasts on top, and keep hot.

4. To the skillet add remaining butter and sauté mushrooms until tender. Spoon over chicken, pour Brown Sauce around the chicken and sprinkle with chopped parsley.

SERVES 4

Tripes à la Mode de Caen
BAKED TRIPE WITH CALVADOS
Awarded the Grand Prix of France in 1958

4 lbs. honeycomb tripe, cut into 2-in. pieces
1 calf's foot, cut into two pieces
1 ox foot, cut into 2 pieces
1 large onion stuck with two cloves
2 diced carrots
1 diced leek
4 cloves crushed garlic
1 large bay leaf
½ teaspoon thyme
4 sprigs parsley
3 stalks diced celery
1 teaspoon crushed peppercorns
1 dash cayenne
2 cups dry white wine
4 cups dry cider
  Water to cover tripe
  Salt and freshly ground black pepper to taste
4 tablespoons Calvados

1. Preheat oven to 350°F.

2. Put the tripe, calf's foot, and ox foot pieces in a big pot. Add enough cold water to cover the tripe and bring to a boil. Simmer for 5 minutes. Drain well.

3. In a square of cheesecloth, bundle together the onion, carrots, leek, garlic, bay leaf, thyme, parsley, celery, and peppercorns. Bring up the ends of the cloth and tie the top with a string to make the bundle.

4. Put tripe, calf's foot and ox foot pieces, the cheesecloth bundle, cayenne, white wine, cider, water to cover tripe, salt, pepper, and 2 tablespoons of Calvados in a big pot. Bring to a boil, take off the stove, and then cover the pot. Seal the edges of the pot with a thick paste made of flour and water; this will seal the pot hermetically so that the aromas do not escape. Bake the tripe 6 to 7 hours.

5. Skim and discard the fat off the cooking broth. Remove and squeeze the cheesecloth bundle to keep all the broth and discard. Remove the calf's foot and ox foot pieces, cutting away the gelatinous skin and discard the bones. Shred the skin and put into the tripe.

6. Bring to a boil one more time and add the remaining Calvados. Serve this dish piping hot.

SERVES 6 TO 8

NOTE: Serve with boiled potatoes and Dijon mustard.

Lapin Diable à la Creme

Awarded the Grand Prix of America in 1959

½ *lb. of butter*
1 *cut-up fresh or frozen rabbit, weighing approx.*
  3½ *lbs.*
4 *shallots, finely chopped*
1 *pint white wine*
1 *pint of cream*
1 *teaspoon of English mustard (powdered)*
2 *pints beef stock*
1 *teaspoon arrowroot*
  Salt and freshly ground pepper to taste
1 *lb. wild rice*
10 *large mushroom heads*
1 *black truffle*
  Croutons

1. Melt ¼ lb. butter in a large pan until it turns to a golden brown. Then place your pieces of rabbit in the butter and sauté them thoroughly on both sides being careful that the flames remain low. Season with salt and pepper to taste.

2. When this has been done sprinkle the finely chopped shallots over the rabbit. Allow to simmer for 5 minutes and then add the white wine. Place a cover over the pan and put it in the oven.

3. When the rabbit has cooked remove the pieces from the sauce and place them where they can be kept warm. Leave the sauce in the pan.

4. Meanwhile, take 1 pint cream and mix with the English mustard and the beef stock, making certain that these ingredients are thoroughly blended. Then add this mixture to your sauce, stirring constantly. Then place the sauce over the flame again and reduce it until the sauce turns to desired consistency.

5. When this has been done, add arrowroot to sauce and stir until sauce has thickened slightly. Then pass the sauce through a piece of fine muslin and then add to it the remaining ¼ lb. butter. Add salt and pepper to taste.

6. Cook the wild rice as you would a rice pilaf and sauté the mushroom heads in butter.

7. In the center of a large round silver platter place the wild rice, pyramid style. Around the wild rice evenly distribute the pieces of rabbit and then spoon the sauce over the rabbit. Place a mushroom head over a piece of rabbit. Over the mushroom place a slice of truffle. Decorate the border of the silver platter with croutons. You are then ready to serve.

SERVES 4

Ossobuco Milanese

3 veal shanks, each sawed into three pieces,
   2 ins. thick
⅓ cup flour
2 teaspoons salt
½ teaspoon freshly ground black pepper
3 tablespoons olive oil
3 tablespoons butter
½ teaspoon ground sage
1 teaspoon rosemary
1 medium-size onion, finely chopped
3 cloves garlic
2 small carrots, diced
1 rib celery, diced
1½ cups dry white wine
1¼ cups chicken stock
2 tablespoons tomato paste
1½ tablespoons chopped parsley
1 tablespoon grated lemon peel

1. Dredge the meat in the flour, which has been seasoned with 1 teaspoon of the salt and the pepper.

2. Heat the oil and butter together in a large skillet. Using medium heat, cook the meat on all sides until golden brown. If necessary, add a little more oil or butter.

3. Arrange the meat in a Dutch oven, standing each piece on its side so the marrow found in the bone does not fall out as the meat cooks. Sprinkle the veal with the sage and rosemary. Add the onion, 1 clove garlic, minced, the carrots and celery. Sprinkle the vegetables with the remaining teaspoon of salt. Cover the Dutch oven closely and braise 10 minutes.

4. Remove the cover and add the wine, chicken stock and tomato paste. Cover and simmer the dish on top of the stove for 2 hours.

5. Mince the remaining 2 cloves of garlic and combine with the parsley and lemon peel. Sprinkle the mixture over the veal and serve immediately.

SERVES 6 TO 8

Cary de Veau
VEAL CURRY

3 lbs. veal, cut in 1½-in. cubes
¼ cup vegetable oil
1 cup sliced carrots
2 diced celery stalks, without leaves
1 large onion, coarsely chopped
2 cups peeled and cubed tart apples
1 banana, peeled and cubed
¼ cup canned sweetened dried coconut
4 cloves garlic, finely chopped
1 large bay leaf
   Pinch of thyme
4 tablespoons curry powder
¼ cup flour
½ cup tomato paste
4 cups chicken or beef broth

½ cup chutney
½ cup heavy cream
   Salt and freshly ground pepper to taste

1. Sauté the veal in a skillet on all sides in half the oil. Put the meat aside. Add remaining oil to the skillet and sauté the carrots, celery, and onions, for 3 to 4 minutes, stirring occasionally.

2. Add the meat, apples, bananas, coconut, garlic, bay leaf, thyme, curry, flour, and tomato paste. Stir well. Add the broth and chutney. Bring to a boil. Cover and bake in a preheated oven at 375° F. for about 1 hour until meat is tender.

3. Remove from the oven and lift the meat with a slotted spoon to a flameproof casserole.

4. Strain the sauce through a china cap or fine sieve. Press with a wooden pestle into a saucepan. Add the meat and bring to a boil. Add the cream and heat through, but do not boil. Serve with rice.

SERVES 8

NOTE: This recipe can be made with lamb.

Veal Shanks à la Française

2 veal shanks
3 tablespoons butter
3 tablespoons peanut oil
¾ cup finely chopped carrots
½ cup finely chopped onion
½ cup finely chopped celery
1 clove garlic, minced
3 sprigs parsley, tied with one bay leaf
  Pinch of thyme
  Salt and freshly ground black pepper to taste
¾ cup dry white wine
1 cup beef broth or consommé
1 cup tinned French peas.

1. Have the butcher slice the veal shanks into 1½-in. rounds, sawing through the bones.

2. Brown the veal rounds on all sides in hot butter and oil. Transfer them to a heavy kettle or Dutch oven. Sprinkle over them the vegetables, seasonings, wine, and beef broth. Cover and cook over low heat until the veal is thoroughly tender, about 2 hours.

3. Transfer the veal to a warm serving platter and cook the liquid in the kettle over high heat until it is reduced slightly. Add the peas, heat through, and pour the sauce over the meat. Serve immediately with noodles or rice.

SERVES 2

Veal Piccata

18 round veal scallops, cut ¼ in. thick
    Flour for dredging
½ cup Butter
    Juice of 2 lemons
  2 tablespoons chopped parsley
    Salt and freshly ground pepper to taste

1. Place the veal scallops between sheets of wax paper and pound them with the flat side of a meat cleaver to make them as thin as possible without breaking through them.

2. Season the scallops with salt and pepper and dust with flour.

3. Heat 3 tablespoons of the butter in a large frying pan over fairly high heat until it is golden, and quickly brown the veal slices, a few at a time, for about 2 minutes on each side.

4. Transfer veal scallops to a hot serving platter to keep warm.

5. Add the lemon juice and parsley to the pan, remove from heat.

6. Swirl in the remaining butter, bit by bit, and pour over the scallops.

SERVES 6

Tournedos Rossini

TOURNEDOS WITH FOIE GRAS AND TRUFFLES

4 slices white bread about ¼ in. thick
4 tablespoons butter
4 6-to 8-oz.tournedos 1½ ins. thick.
  Salt and freshly ground black pepper to taste
4 round slices foie gras ¼ in. thick
4 round slices truffle ⅛ in. thick
½ cup Madeira wine
1 tablespoon truffle juice
1 cup Brown Sauce (see page 66)

1. Cut the bread slices into 2½-in.-diameter rounds, then sauté them in a skillet with 1 tablespoon of butter until golden brown on both sides. Set croutons aside.

2. Heat 2 tablespoons of butter in a skillet, season the tournedos with salt and pepper, then sauté them for 3 to 4 minutes on each side, or until they are cooked according to your taste.

3. On a platter first place the croutons, on top of that put the tournedos, then foie gras, lastly the truffles. Keep them warm.

4. Remove the fat from the skillet and add the Madeira wine, truffle juice, and Brown Sauce. Stir with a wire whisk for 2 to 3 minutes over very low heat. Strain the sauce through a fine sieve and put in a small saucepan. Cut the remaining tablespoon of butter into small pieces and swirl into the sauce.

5. Correct seasoning if necessary, then pour sauce over the tournedos and serve very hot.

SERVES 4

Filet of Beef Wellington

12 oz. flour
½ teaspoon salt
6 oz. butter
6 oz. shortening
3 egg yolks
1 cup cold water
5 lbs. whole beef tenderloin, trimmed and peeled
8 oz. liver pate or foie gras
2 oz. finely chopped truffle peelings
6 oz. chopped and sautéd mushrooms

1. To make the dough, first sift the flour and then add the salt, butter, shortening, egg yolks, and water. Blend the ingredients lightly.

2. Cover the dough with a cloth and allow to stand for 1 hour.

3. Sear tenderloin well, leaving center practically raw.

4. Cool the tenderloin and spread with liver pate or foie gras. Add the sautéed mushrooms and sprinkle the truffles.

5. Roll out the dough to ³⁄16 in. thick

6. Wrap dough around tenderloin keeping seam on the bottom. Fold ends under, decorate with cutouts from dough trims, and then brush with egg wash.

7. Place on an oiled sheet and bake in 375° F. oven for 40 minutes or until the dough is done. If dough browns too quickly, shield with foil.

8. Serve one slice per person. Cut slices ¾ in. thick. Serve this dish with Madeira Sauce (see page 123) with chopped truffles, served separately in a gravy dish.

SERVES 8

Beef Strogonoff

1 tablespoon butter
½ tablespoon finely chopped shallots
1 tablespoon finely chopped onion
12 fresh mushrooms, sliced
1 tablespoon flour
1 tablespoon white vinegar
1 tablespoon dry white wine
2 tablespoons Sherry
1 teaspoon paprika
3 cups sour cream
1 cup heavy cream
1½ tablespoons vegetable oil
1¼ lbs. tenderloin or sirloin beef, cut into strips 2 ins.
     long and ½ in. thick
     Salt and freshly ground black pepper to taste
1 tablespoon julienne-cut sour pickles
1 teaspoon chopped chives

1. Melt butter in a saucepan and sauté shallots, onions, and mushrooms for 2 to 3 minutes; add the flour, mix well, and simmer for 1 more minute. Add the vinegar, white wine, Sherry, paprika, 2 cups sour cream, and heavy cream, stirring until the sauce thickens.

2. In a separate pan heat oil and add the meat. Season with salt and pepper and brown the meat quickly on both sides.

3. Remove meat from the pan; add meat to the sauce. Then add pickles and chopped chives. Simmer until the meat is tender, without allowing sauce to boil. Add 1 cup sour cream and mix thoroughly. Serve this dish with wild rice.

SERVES 4

SAUCES

Sauce Diable

2 shallots, finely chopped
2 tablespoons coarsely chopped onions
1 clove garlic, finely chopped
15 crushed peppercorns
    Pinch of thyme
½ bay leaf
¼ cup red wine vinegar
1 cup Brown Sauce (see page 66)
2 tablespoons white wine
1 tablespoon imported Dijon mustard
1 teaspoon chopped parsley
1 drop Tabasco
    Salt to taste

1. Cook shallots, onions, garlic, peppercorns, thyme, bay leaf, and wine vinegar in a small saucepan until almost all the liquid has evaporated. Add the Brown Sauce and let simmer for a couple of minutes.

2. Strain the mixture through a sieve, pushing as much of the solids through as possible. Return to the heat and bring to a boil.

3. Remove the sauce from the heat and stir in the butter, mustard, chopped parsley, and Tabasco.

4. Serve with broiled chicken, Rock Cornish hen, Royal Squab, or squab chicken.

YIELDS 1 CUP

Curry Sauce

4½ tablespoons butter
1 clove garlic, finely minced
⅓ cup finely chopped onion
⅓ cup finely chopped celery
3 tablespoons chopped carrot
2 tablespoons flour
2 tablespoons curry powder
½ bay leaf
2 sprigs parsley
2 sprigs fresh thyme or ½ teaspoon dried
1¾ cups chicken broth
    Salt and freshly ground pepper to taste

1. Heat 3 tablespoons of butter in a saucepan and add the garlic, onion, celery, and carrot. Cook, stirring, until onion is wilted. Add the flour and cook, stirring, about 3 minutes. Stir in the curry, bay leaf, parsley, and thyme.

2. Using a wire whisk, continue to stir briskly while adding the broth. Simmer, covered, stirring occasionally, about 30 minutes. Put the mixture, including soft vegetables, through a fine sieve, using a wooden spoon. Swirl in the remaining butter and add salt and pepper to taste.

YIELDS ABOUT 1½ CUPS

Sauce Piquante

2 tablespoons mustard, Dijon or Dusseldorf
3 tablespoons bottled Sauce Robert
4 tablespoons Sauce Diable (see page 121)
¼ teaspoon Worcestershire sauce
¼ teaspoon Tabasco sauce
1¼ cups heavy cream
    Salt and freshly ground pepper to taste

In a saucepan, combine all the ingredients. Simmer, stirring occasionally, about 10 minutes.

YIELDS ABOUT 1½ CUPS

Madeira Sauce

> 3 tablespoons butter
> 2 tablespoons finely chopped shallots
> 1½ cups Brown Sauce (see page 66)
> 1 tablespoon chopped canned truffles with their liquid
> ¼ cup Madeira wine

1. Melt 2 tablespoons of butter in a saucepan and sauté the shallots for 2 minutes over moderate heat.

2. Add the Brown Sauce and truffles with the liquid. Let it boil. Then add the Madeira and let simmer for 2 to 3 minutes.

3. Remove from heat and add the remaining 1 tablespoon of butter. Stir gently and then serve.

YIELDS 1½ CUPS

Apple Sauce for Broiled Baby Turkey

> 2 tablespoons fresh grated horseradish
> 6 tablespoons applesauce
> 1 teaspoon Worcestershire sauce
> 4 tablespoons heavy cream
> 1 teaspoon paprika
> 1 drop Tabasco
> Salt and freshly ground pepper to taste

In a bowl, combine all the ingredients and mix well. Heat lightly and serve on the side.

SERVES 4

Mayonnaise for Cold Salmon

2 egg yolks
1 tablespoon vinegar
1 teaspoon Dijon mustard
   Salt and white pepper to taste
½ cup of vegetable oil

1. Put the egg yolks in a bowl and add the vinegar, mustard, salt, and pepper. Mix them together thoroughly.

2. Add the oil very gradually drop by drop, stirring continually with a wire whisk. When the mayonnaise starts to thicken stop adding the oil and add 1 tablespoon of hot water. Stir it thoroughly before continuing to add oil.

SERVES 4

NOTE: All ingredients and utensils must be slightly warm.

Rouille

GARLIC MAYONNAISE FOR BOUILLABAISE OR FISH SOUP

2 egg yolks
1½ tablespoons crushed garlic
   Pulp of 1 small baked potato (about 2 tablespoons)
½ teaspoon paprika
1 tablespoon crushed hot red pepper
1 dash cayenne
   Salt and freshly ground pepper to taste
1 tablespoon lemon juice
1½ cups olive oil
   Tabasco to taste

1. Put egg yolks in a mixing bowl. Add garlic, potato, paprika, hot red pepper, cayenne, salt, pepper, lemon juice, and Tabasco.

2. Beat with a wire whisk until it becomes a smooth paste. Gradually add olive oil until the mixture thickens (do not overbeat).

YIELDS 2 CUPS

DESSERTS

Beignets Soufflés with Sabayon Sauce
CREAM PUFF FRITTER

1 cup milk
½ stick sweet butter
1 tablespoon sugar
½ teaspoon vanilla extract
1 cup flour
4 eggs
5 cups vegetable oil
   Powdered sugar

1. Combine the milk, butter, sugar, and vanilla in a saucepan and bring to a boil. When mixture is boiling, add the flour all at once. Mix well, rapidly, with a wooden spatula until mixture separates from side of the pan. Continue cooking and stirring the mixture for about 1 minute.

2. Transfer the mixture to a clean bowl and let cool for 5 minutes. Add 1 egg at a time, stirring the mixture until thoroughly blended. Cover the dough with an oiled piece of wax paper and put it in the refrigerator until ready to use. It should be cool when used.

3. Heat the oil to 350°F. Scoop up about ¾ tablespoon of dough, and with your index finger, push the mixture to the edge of the spoon. Let it drop into the hot oil, but work close to the oil to prevent splashing.

4. Let the fritters cook for about 6 to 7 minutes at the same temperature. The balls will float to the top and turn around by themselves as they brown and expand. Remove the balls from the oil and drain on paper towels. They should be very light and delicate.

5. Arrange the fritters on a serving dish. Sprinkle generously with powdered sugar and serve with Sabayon Sauce (see page 126).

SERVES 8

Sabayon

6 egg yolks
2 whole eggs
½ cup granulated sugar
½ cup Marsala or sweet Sherry
¼ cup brandy or rum
Pinch of cinnamon
½ teaspoon vanilla

1. Place egg yolks and whole eggs in top of a deep 2-qt. enamel double boiler and beat with a rotary beater until light, about 3 minutes.

2. Gradually beat in granulated sugar. Add, little by little, Marsala or sherry, then brandy or rum, and flavor with cinnamon and vanilla. (At this point the mixture will not be as thick as before, but this is all right.)

3. Place pan over boiling water and continue beating with rotary beater until it foams way up almost to the top of the pan, about 3 to 4 minutes. Be careful not to overcook.

4. Remove from heat and continue beating with a spoon, scraping the thickest part into the rest until smooth.

5. Pour immediately into 8 glasses or custard cups of ½-cup capacity. Cool and refrigerate until ready to serve, at least 2 hours.

SERVES 8

NOTE: Can be used as a topping for fresh strawberries, raspberries, blueberries, and other fruits, and as a sauce for Beignets Soufflés.

Chocolate Mousse

3 oz. grated sweet chocolate
3 oz. grated unsweetened chocolate
¼ cup water
4 egg yolks
4 egg whites
¾ cup sugar
2 cups whipped heavy cream
4 oz. rum
2 tablespoons crushed roasted hazelnuts

1. Melt the chocolate in the water using a double boiler. Remove from heat and place on ice to cool, stirring from time to time.

2. When mixture starts to set, add yolks and blend well.

3. Beat egg whites until stiff, adding sugar gradually. Fold gently into the yolk mixture, alternating with the whipped cream, rum, and hazelnuts.

4. Pour into individual cups. Chill 2 to 3 hours and serve.

SERVES 6

Hire French Master Chef:

Stop & Shop To Sell Ready-Made Foods, Packaged But Not Frozen, In All Stores

Jean Vergnes, famous French chef, has left the position as executive chef at New York City's Colony Restaurant to accept a similar position with Stop & Shop. Vergnes and his team of chefs will prepare some 30 ready-to-eat foods for sale by the food chain, starting in mid-January. The food will be packaged but not frozen. Vergnes is shown ready to begin a day's work.

Stop & Shop will introduce by mid-January a new line of some 30 ready-to-eat foods prepared in special kitchens off Route 128 at Readville, Mass. The packaged but non-frozen food will be sold in special departments to be set up in all of the food chain's 150 stores.

The food will be prepared under the supervision of Jean Vergnes, engaged by Stop & Shop as executive chef. The French born and trained Vergnes joins the Boston-based company from the Colony Restaurant in New York.

Vergnes listed some of the special foods he will prepare while in New Haven Tuesday. Among them are beef stroganoff, beef goulash, chickie currie, Chicken cacciatore, chicken and wine sauce, veal marsala, spaghetti and meat sauce, spaghetti and meat balls, American, German and French potato salad, cole slaw, beet and onion salad, lobster Newburgh, clam sauce, tapioca, rice and grape nut puddings and many others.

Vergnes was awarded the Grand Prize in France in 1958 and in the United States in 1959. He commanded the kitchen at the Colony, a famous restaurant that once prompted Jimmy Walker (then Mayor of New York City) to make the Colony easily accessible to his Rolls-Royce by chang-ing the direction of traffic on its street.

Long Experience

A culinary expert with 27 years experience, Vergnes is a naturalized American citizen. Born in Deauphine, near Grenoble, France he began his culinary career in 1935 in the employ of father of C. C. Philippe of Waldorf-Astoria fame, at the Restaurant Philippe, Grenoble. After a two-year apprenticeship there, he went to Paris where, with an interruption for war duty, he served four years as assistant chef.

Some of the famous European restaurants and hotels at which Vergenes was employed are Le Perigord and La Cigogne Restaurants and the Hotel Majestic and the Hotel Raphael, all in Paris and the Belle Terrasse Restaurant at Tivoli Gardens, Denmark. He has also worked at the Castle Harbor Hotel, Bermuda.

Vergnes launched his culinary career in the United States on Oct. 4, 1950, at the Waldorf-Astoria. Before joining the Colony as saucier in 1951, he worked at La Vie En Rose. In 1952 he was appointed executive chef at the Colony.

Served Famous

During his time at the Colony Chef Vergnes has served many important personages some of whom have been President and Mrs. Kennedy, Prince Ranier and Princess Grace, former Postmaster General James Farley, the Shah of Iran and Krishna Mennon, then India's delegate to the United Nations.

In re-counting his long and interesting career, Vergnes recalls the time when Danny Kaye came into his Colony kitchen to "teach" him how to cook. Probably the most startling experience was the time a waiter got mixed up and put Hollandaise Sauce on dessert for topping, and put the dessert topping on an order of asparagus.

"Both must have been tasty," says Vergnes, "because both were eaten without complaints."

The Boston Herald *piece that ran when I took the job at Stop & Shop Inc.*

V

COMMERCIAL VENTURES

In 1962 Craig Claiborne ran an article in the New York *Times* commenting on the recent movement of top restaurant chefs to positions within large food industries. In the article he mentioned Pierre Franey's decision to leave Le Pavillon restaurant to join the Howard Johnson's restaurant chain. He also mentioned my departure from The Colony to join Stop & Shop as executive chef for the Boston chain.

Some may ask why two chefs whose specialty is haute cuisine would ever decide to leave their positions to pursue such commercial endeavors. In my case, there were several reasons for the move. First, aside from my brief experience at the Waldorf-Astoria, all my training and knowledge was tied to the French restaurant system. Once I made the decision to stay in America, I realized that I had much to learn about this country's standard food habits. I had matured a great deal since first coming to America and I realized Stop & Shop would be a great opportunity to acquire more knowledge of the way Americans operated their food businesses.

Second, although I would have liked to have started my own restaurant after leaving The Colony, no viable situation presented itself. In many ways I am grateful I didn't get involved in any restaurant venture at that time because the restaurant business was taking a real beating. Costs kept spiraling—not only the cost of food but also wages. Both the cooks union and dining-room employees had won contractual concessions. The 1960s were a restaurateur's nightmare. And this is what led to the downfall of such great eating institutions as The Colony, Le Pavillon, Café Chauveron, Brussel and others. In the back of my mind, I knew that one day I would own my own place. This had been my dream since childhood. But I also knew that I needed to be patient and wait until the right conditions presented themselves.

A third important consideration in taking the job was my family. By 1958 I was legally divorced from my wife, Jeannine. For all intents and purposes our marriage had ended three years prior. I was devoting just about all of my waking time to The Colony, and it really took its toll on our relationship. However, in 1959, I married my second wife, Pauline. I had met her when I accompanied my good friend Raymond Richez up to Haines Falls, in the Catskills of New York. There was a place up there called La Cascade where a lot of the French people would meet on weekends. On one of those weekends Raymond introduced me to Pauline, a beautiful French-Canadian woman. It's hard for me to put into words what I felt for her, but I can assure you it felt like we had always known each other. I just knew I wanted to marry her.

In 1961, just before leaving The Colony, our first child, Robert, was born. Two years later, our second child, Roger, was born. It seemed clear to me that if I was going to get a chance to watch my children grow I had better take a job that offered me the kind of hours most people are used to. At The Colony I worked a sixteen- to eighteen-hour day, six days a week, for twelve years. This obviously afforded me little or no time to spend with my wife and children. At Stop & Shop I would work an eight-hour day, and only five days a week. So, although my income dropped to fifty percent of what it had been previously, the job was much more conducive to having a family life.

I am very proud of what I accomplished during the brief time I worked at Stop & Shop. The company constructed a new building in Dedham, Massachusetts, that was specifically designed for me and my fellow workers. There, I was asked to develop a food line called the Caterer Kitchen, which was designed to be a fresh-food line with a short shelf life. The idea was to make available to shoppers ready-to-eat fresh meals that they could just take home, heat up and serve. I developed well over a hundred such recipes for this line. Unfortunately, I think that in 1963 the idea was simply too far ahead of its time. One must remember that in the 1960s women made up only a small part of the work force. I think many families were still having meals prepared at home by mother. It's really only been in recent years, with the growing trend of both husband and wife working, that we've seen growth in take-out and ready-to-eat foods in the super-markets. Moreover, consumers in the Boston area were just not ready to compromise their buying habits for the pricier Caterer Kitchen line. I think the line would have had much more success in a cosmopolitan area such as New York. I say that the line was ahead of its time because today, when I go to the supermarket with my wife, all I see are countless brands of both frozen and fresh ready-to-cook meals. The Caterer Kitchen may not have succeeded, but I like to think that it helped usher in and pave the way for many of the food lines we see in supermarkets today.

The two years I spent with Stop & Shop were, overall, a very positive experience. I never had any intention of staying with the company for long, but it was most certainly an invaluable business experience. Aside from the opportunity to experiment with new concepts in the presentation of dishes, it afforded me a closer look at how Americans operate their food business. My one criticism of the individuals who ran Stop & Shop, and companies like it, is that, at the time, they simply did not employ enough qualified people. They tended to overcompensate one knowledgeable vice president and assume his acumen would somehow filter down through the lower ranks. The problem was that because the lower ranks drew modest salaries, they were not always made up of people who could benefit from the knowledge given them.

I think what is needed in these large food companies is a greater number of qualified professionals working at every level, from clerk to upper management. When this occurs, the company structure will be a much more unified one. It will also be more effective in meeting the ever-changing demands of the consumer, and perhaps even in staying one step ahead of it. The analogy I draw here is to that of the French kitchen, for in the kitchen it is not just the chef who knows what he is doing and what is going on, but each and every member of his crew as well. This kind of cohesiveness is what breeds quality and productivity, and American food companies would do well to nurture it.

I am presently serving as a food consultant for a New Jersey–based pasta manufacturer named Famiglia Industries. My official title is Vice President–Product Development, which is really just a fancy way of saying chef. If someone had told me while I was growing up in France that I would one day work as a consultant, developing formulas and recipes for a pasta manufacturer, I would have told him he was crazy. But the unpredictable course my life has taken is a testament to what I love so much about this country. It is a place where new, unguessed-at opportunities present themselves every day.

I came to this country just as Americans were starting to learn about French and gourmet foods. The knowledge that I and many of my confreres possessed made us very attractive to large food industries that wanted to better their products. At Famiglia I have been able to create a great number of innovative recipes and formulas, all of which stress the freshness so vital to any dish. Among them are fresh vegetable pastas made of carrots, broccoli and spinach; frozen pastas concocted of cheese, meat, tofu and soy protein fillings; five different types of sauces; eight varieties of dry pasta; and a special line of vitamin-fortified pasta. I have also put together a tofu-based filling that we intend to use in a pasta assortment called Tofu Classics. The line will be a mix of tofu-filled ravioli, manicotti, stuffed shells and crêpes.

Some may still ask, What is a French chef with my classic Escoffian background doing experimenting with tofu and soy protein fillings? My reply to them is simple: Escoffier lived in a different age. We are now in the 1980s. As a chef one must work with science and food products to integrate them with a knowledge of the present. Just as Escoffier modified French food in his era to reflect ideas about health that were prevalent at the time, I, too, feel that it is a responsibility of those in my trade to find products that respond to the new information about health and nutrition that is being gleaned every day.

Preparing a cheese ravioli recipe at Famiglia.

I don't feel I have lowered my standard of quality because I work for a large manufacturer as opposed to an exclusive French restaurant. If anything, I would like to believe that I have raised the standard of quality in the recipes and formulas I created at Famiglia and Stop & Shop. I have always used natural spices and natural preservatives in all of my canned, packaged and frozen creations.

Famiglia now has over twenty-one new products, all with a shelf life of over six months. Our first national market breakthrough came in the fall of 1986, when Campbell Soups selected two recipes for their line—a meat tortellini and cheese-stuffed shells—that were created by me and a fellow worker, Jean Danet. General Foods' Ronzoni division has also recently picked up our pasta products for national marketing.

Right now I am working on a rather interesting project, trying to develop a Kosher pasta line. I was on hand at a recent kosher convention, held at the Jacob Javits Convention Center in New York

City, at which Jean Danet and I were at the Famiglia booth, serving scores of interested consumers samples of our unique kosher pasta. This would be a great market to tap, and by the reaction we received, I think it could be tapped fairly easily.

The two constraints I've found while working at Famiglia that most influence the manner in which I prepare things are the pricing of the product and the actual machinery used in mass production. Often, I have wanted to use more meat in the tortellini, or cheese in the ravioli. But because of the constraints placed on me by management to reduce the cost of the product, I've had to compromise. The huge machinery used in making many of the pastas has also presented problems. These machines, though highly efficient at turning out great numbers of a product, quickly create much spoilage because of their indelicacy. In the commercial world the machines are the bosses because they dictate what a chef can and cannot do. So, I have often had to accept, say, a ravioli or tortellini that is not as refined as if it were prepared by hand. But, I will say that the industry is working on this, and I believe that it won't be too long before we have a machine that will be able to prepare food with refinement and still maintain great output.

I have always been one to pursue new and different endeavors, for I have learned that despite first impressions and outward appearances, these endeavors usually afford me the opportunity to make a difference in what I do for a living. Unlike many of the top French chefs who felt I was compromising my French culinary background by getting involved with Stop & Shop and Famiglia, I found these experiences to be, without question, positive ones. I have gained a better awareness of Americans and their food habits. Moreover, my tenure at Stop & Shop and Famiglia has made me a better business-man, since in my capacity as a consultant I've been responsible for million-dollar budgets. After spending twenty-nine years in the restaurant business prior to my experience at Stop & Shop—and fifty years before coming to Famiglia—I have come to realize that there will always be more for me to learn and master in my chosen trade.

Overall, these ventures have given me the opportunity to *truly* diversify my culinary skills, something I never would have been able to do if I had stayed in the restaurant system I knew so well. In 1971

I did return to the French restaurant system to work as the executive chef at Maxwell's Plum, and in 1974 I opened Le Cirque in the capacity of restaurateur. I make the distinction between chef and restaurateur because it underlines the significance of my commercial ventures. Every one of the experiences in my life has been like a stop at yet another station in the kitchen, and each stop has contributed to my forming a more complete approach to, and comprehensive understanding of, cuisine in general.

APPETIZERS

Manhattan Clam Chowder

2 dozen medium-size hard clams
2 cups cold water
  Pinch of dried thyme
½ bay leaf
2 oz. lean slab bacon, sliced ¼ in. thick and diced
    into ¼ in. pieces
1 medium onion, chopped very fine
1 tablespoon chopped leeks
1 clove garlic, chopped fine
1 tablespoon diced celery
½ tablespoon diced carrots
½ tablespoon diced green peppers
1 large tomato, diced
2 medium potatoes, diced
  Salt and freshly ground black pepper to taste
1 teaspoon chopped parsley
  Drops of Worcestershire sauce
  Drops of Tabasco sauce
1 tablespoon butter

1. Wash the clams throughly. Place them in a saucepan with the water, thyme, and bay leaf. Bring to a boil and let that cook slowly for 5 to 6 minutes, or until the shells open.

2. Strain the clam broth through a very fine sieve and reserve. Remove clams from the shells. Clean and chop coarsely.

3. Sauté the bacon in a saucepan. Add the clam broth, onions, leek, garlic, celery, carrots, green pepper, and tomatoes. Cook slowly for about 10 minutes.

4. Add the potatoes. Season with salt and freshly ground black pepper, and cook until potatoes are done.

5. Remove from heat and add the clams, chopped parsley, Worcestershire sauce, Tabasco, and butter. Serve hot.

SERVES 4

Smoked Cod Chowder

1 small onion, diced
1 leek, diced
2 celery stalks, diced
1 medium carrot, diced
1 large potato, diced
1 tomato, peeled and diced
2 slices bacon
6 ounces smoked codfish, diced
6 cups water
½ tablespoon butter
  Pinch of thyme
  Pinch of salt and freshly ground pepper

1. In a large pot add all ingredients except the potatoes and codfish. Simmer on a low flame for about 5 minutes.

2. Add the water and bring to a boil, then add the potatoes and codfish. Let cook for about a half hour on low heat. Season to taste with salt and pepper.

SERVES 4

NOTE: Serve with crackers or slice of toasted roll.

Tomato Soup

1½ sticks butter
1 large onion, thinly sliced
½ teaspoon dried thyme
½ teaspoon dried basil
   Salt and freshly ground pepper to taste
1 2-lb., 3 oz. can of Italian imported tomatoes (or
   fresh tomatoes)
3 tablespoons tomato paste
¼ cup flour
3 ¾ cups beef or chicken broth
1 teaspoon sugar
2 cups heavy cream
   Croutons for garnish

1. Melt 1 stick butter in a large kettle. Add onion, thyme, basil, salt, and pepper. Cook, stirring occasionally, until onion is wilted.

2. Add tomatoes, which have been puréed through a food mill, and tomato paste and stir to blend. Simmer 10 minutes.

3. Place flour in a small mixing bowl and add about 5 tablespoons of broth, stirring to blend. Stir this into the tomato mixture. Add the remaining chicken broth and simmer 30 minutes, stirring frequently from the bottom of the kettle so the soup doesn't stick or burn.

4. Blend soup in blender. Return to heat and add sugar and cream. Simmer, stirring occasionally, for 5 minutes; add the remaining butter, swirling it around in the soup.

SERVES 6

Oysters Rockefeller

3 cups milk
4 tablespoons flour
4 tablespoons butter
3 dozen raw oysters in the shell
½ cup white wine
4 shallots
1½ lbs. chopped fresh spinach, cooked
1 cup kernel corn (canned or frozen)
1 cup heavy cream
4 egg yolks
½ cup Parmesan cheese

1. Make a cream sauce by mixing the milk, flour, and butter. Set aside.

2. Open the oysters and remove them from their shells (save the shells), and place oysters in saucepan. Poach oysters in their own juice, barely bringing to a boil.

3. Remove oysters, reserving the juice, and then simmer the juice until slightly reduced. Add the white wine and reduce again.

4. Sauté chopped shallots in a skillet, add the cooked chopped spinach, and add the kernel corn.

5. Place a spoonful of the spinach mixture in each oyster shell. Place an oyster on top of each, and top with more spinach mixture.

6. To the cream sauce, add the reserved oyster juice, heavy cream, and lightly beaten egg yolks. Stir in a double boiler until thickened.

7. Spoon this sauce on each oyster, and sprinkle with Parmesan cheese.

8. Place under broiler until lightly browned.

SERVES 6

Norway Sardines Mimosa

1 teaspoon lemon juice
1 tablespoon sour cream
1 teaspoon imported French mustard
1 tablespoon mayonnaise
1 teaspoon finely chopped onion or shallot
*　Salt and freshly ground black pepper to taste*
*　Dash of Tabasco and Worcestershire sauces*
4 slices of toast
2 fresh tomatoes, sliced
2 3¾-oz. cans Norway sardines
1 hard-boiled egg, sieved
8 stuffed olives, sliced

1. Thoroughly mix lemon juice, sour cream, mustard, mayonnaise, onion, salt, pepper, and Tabasco and Worcestershire sauces.

2. Spread mixture on toast. Top with sliced tomatoes, then with sardines. Sprinkle with sieved egg and top with olive slices. Cut in triangles and serve.

SERVES 4

Caesar Salad

*　Salt and freshly ground pepper to taste*
1 clove garlic, peeled and crushed
1 teaspoon prepared Dijon mustard
1½ tablespoons lemon juice or wine vinegar
3½ tablespoons olive oil
2 bunches romaine
2 tablespoons grated Parmesan cheese
1 can anchovies, drained (cut optional)
2 eggs, boiled for one minute
1 cup croutons

1. Sprinkle the bottom of a wooden salad bowl with salt and black pepper. Mix it with the garlic. Add the mustard and lemon juice (or wine vinegar) with a wooden spoon until the salt dissolves.

2. Add the olive oil and stir rapidly until the liquid is blended.

3. Wash the romaine well, and dry the leaves with a towel. Tear the leaves into bite-size pieces and add this to the salad bowl. Sprinkle the parmeasan cheese, add the anchovies, and break the eggs over the salad.

4. Sprinkle the croutons (bread cubes toasted lightly in olive oil) and mix gently, but thoroughly, with wooden fork and spoon.

SERVES 6

PASTAS

Pasta with Clams and Basil

1 lb. fettuccine or linguini

1½ lbs. large ripe tomatoes (3 or 4), seeded and
    chopped

2 garlic cloves, finely chopped

2 tablespoons chopped fresh basil

1 tablespoon chopped Italian parsley

¼ cup olive oil

Salt and freshly ground pepper to taste

18 medium-sized cherrystone clams, shucked and
    coarsely chopped

1. Cook pasta in a large pot of boiling salted water for about 8
minutes, until al dente.

2. While pasta is cooking, sauté chopped garlic with olive oil for a
couple of minutes, add the chopped tomatoes, basil, parsley, and
chopped clams with their juice. Let simmer for 1 minute; add salt
and black pepper.

3. Drain the pasta and toss it with the clam sauce and serve.

SERVES 4 TO 6

Fettuccine Alfredo

1 lb. spinach or white fettuccine
1½ cups heavy cream
⅓ cup chicken broth
4 tablespoons sweet butter
2 egg yolks, lightly beaten
4 slices prosciutto, cut julienne style
½ cup grated Parmesan cheese
Salt and freshly ground black pepper to taste
½ lb. sliced fresh mushrooms
1 pinch nutmeg

1. In a skillet, lightly sauté the prosciutto and mushrooms in butter.

2. Add the heavy cream, chicken broth, egg yolk, and nutmeg.

3. In the meantime, boil the pasta al dente.

4. Drain pasta thoroughly and place in the heavy cream.

5. Mix and stir until pasta is well coated.

6. Season with salt and black pepper to taste.

7. Add Parmesan cheese and serve.

SERVES 6

Fettuccine Bolognese

2½ oz. prosciutto, chopped
3 tablespoons olive oil
2 garlic cloves, chopped
1 small onion, chopped
1 small carrot, chopped
1 stick celery, chopped
10 oz. ground beef
4 oz. mild Italian sausage
2 oz. dried mushrooms, soaked for 20 minutes,
    drained and rinsed
½ cup red wine
1 tablespoon chopped fresh parsley
½ teaspoon dried marjoram
¼ teaspoon grated nutmeg
    Salt and freshly ground black pepper to taste
½ tablespoon all-purpose flour
10 oz. canned tomatoes drained and puréed
1 tablespoon tomato paste
1 lb. fettuccine
    Grated Parmesan cheese to taste

1. Sauté the prosciutto gently in the oil, then add garlic, onions, carrot, and celery and sauté for about 2 minutes. Add the beef, sausage, and mushrooms, stir carefully, and cook for about 20 minutes (add a little stock or water to prevent drying). Add wine and herbs, and season with salt and pepper. Stir a few minutes, then add the flour, mixing with care. Add the tomatoes and tomato paste. Cook, stirring for a few minutes, then cover and leave to simmer for about 1 hour.

2. While sauce is cooking, boil fettuccine in plenty of salted water until al dente. Drain and pour into warmed bowl. Pour sauce over pasta, mix together, sprinkle with Parmesan, and serve.

SERVES 4 TO 6

Cheese Tortellini Salad Riviera

1 lb. cheese tortellini
½ cup diced sweet red pimentos
½ cup diced green peppers
8 black olives, sliced
2 tablespoons chopped Italian parsley
½ cup crushed walnuts
½ cup prosciutto, cut into strips 1 in. long
1½ cups diced fresh tomato
1 tablespoon chopped fresh basil

Dressing:

2 tablespoons Dijon mustard
6 tablespoons olive oil
3 tablespoons red wine vinegar
3 tablespoons mayonnaise
3 cloves garlic, chopped very fine
Salt and freshly ground black pepper to taste.

1. Cook cheese tortellini in a large pot of boiling salted water until al dente. Rinse in cold water, drain.

2. Mix pimentos, green peppers, black olives, parsley, walnuts, prosciutto, tomato, and basil.

3. Combine dressing ingredients, beat well with a wire whisk, and add to salad. Toss very well and chill.

SERVES 8

ENTRÉES

Poulet de Paris

SAUTÉED CHICKEN WITH CREAM AND FRESH MUSHROOM SAUCE

1 3-lb. roasting chicken
Salt and freshly ground pepper to taste
2 tablespoons butter or margarine
½ lb. fresh mushrooms, sliced
1 small onion, chopped
½ cup dry sherry or dry white wine
2 egg yolks
1 pint heavy cream
Pinch of chopped parsley

1. Cut chicken into 8 pieces. Season with salt and pepper. Melt butter in a deep skillet and cook chicken over fairly high heat, turning pieces to brown on all sides.

2. Turn the heat down to medium, cover skillet and simmer 7 to 8 minutes.

3. Add the chopped mushrooms and onions and cover again, cooking it gently for another 10 minutes. Add the wine and continue cooking gently, with the pot covered, for 5 minutes.

4. When the chicken is well cooked, place pieces on serving platter, keeping it hot.

5. Lightly stir the egg yolks and heavy cream into the liquid in the skillet. Simmer sauce for about 4 to 5 minutes, but do not boil. Correct seasoning.

6. Pour this sauce over the chicken and sprinkle with parsley. Serve on fresh hot toast triangles.

SERVES 4

Lobster Newburg

4 lobsters, 1¼ lbs. each (or 2 lobsters, 2½ lbs. each)
1½ tablespoons butter
¼ teaspoon salt
¼ teaspoon white pepper
1 teaspoon paprika
½ cup Sherry wine
3 cups cream, heavy or light
4 egg yolks, slightly beaten

1. Cook lobsters in boiling water and remove meat from shell. Cut meat into bite size pieces.

2. Sauté the lobster meat with butter in skillet, season with salt, pepper, and paprika. Simmer for a few minutes.

3. Add the Sherry and simmer to reduce the liquid by about half.

4. Mix egg yolks with cream and add to lobster mixture. Stir gently until mixture starts to thicken. Do not overcook.

SERVES 4

Swedish Meat Balls

2 tablespoons butter
3 tablespoons minced onion
1 cup fresh bread crumbs
1 cup milk (or equal parts milk and cream)
¾ lb. ground round
¼ lb. ground veal
¼ lb. ground pork
1 egg
　Salt and freshly ground pepper to taste
　Chopped fresh parsley
¼ cup flour
¾ cup cream or milk

1. Melt butter and sauté onions until golden brown.

2. Soak bread crumbs in milk, add meat, egg, onion, salt, pepper and parsley and mix thoroughly.

3. Shape into balls about 1½ in. in diameter and roll in flour. Reserve 1 tablespoon of flour.

4. Melt enough additional butter in skillet to cover bottom of pan and brown meat balls over medium heat. Shake pan occasionally to keep round shape of meat balls. Remove to serving dish and keep warm.

5. Combine reserved flour with cream and stir gradually into pan juices, using wire whisk. Simmer for 5 minutes, stirring occasionally. Pour gravy over meat balls and serve hot.

SERVES 6

DESSERTS

Fruit Cake

10 oz. cake flour
8 oz. sweet butter
1 teaspoon baking powder
1 teaspoon vanilla or lemon extract
1 cup whole eggs
8 oz. sugar
1/4 teaspoon salt
3 oz. light corn syrup
1/3 cup milk
7 oz. raisins
7 oz. mixed diced candied fruits
3 oz. chopped walnuts

1. In large bowl combine the cake flour, butter, baking powder, and vanilla. Whip until light and fluffy.

2. In a separate bowl whip together the eggs, sugar and salt. Then lightly fold this mixture into the flour mixture. Do not overmix.

3. Again in a separate bowl mix the syrup and milk and slowly add to the batter until thoroughly mixed.

4. Lightly dust the raisins, candied fruit, and chopped walnuts with flour, then fold into the batter.

5. Pour the batter into a greased loaf pan (2 small ones or 1 large.) Bake for 1 hour at 350° F. When the top of the cake feels solid, the cake is done.

SERVES 8

Floating Island

Meringue:

> 8 egg whites
> 12 oz. sugar

1. Beat egg whites until they start to stiffen. Slowly add the sugar.

2. Heat water in a deep pan until warm to the touch. Then scoop the egg white mixture into the water. Cook for 1½ to 2 minutes on each side.

3. Remove the egg white and put on a cooking sheet. Cover with granulated sugar. Brown under broiler. Serve with Sauce Anglaise. (See below)

SERVES 10

Sauce Anglaise

> 1 quart milk
> 6 egg yolks
> 8 oz. sugar
> Liquor to taste, such as Grand Marnier

1. Add 6 oz. of sugar to the milk, and boil. Let the milk rest.

2. Mix the remainder of the sugar to the egg yolks.

3. Add 1 cup of boiled milk to the sugar and egg mixture. Add the rest of the milk to the mixture. Cook for less than a minute. Add the liquor to the mixture.

4. In a cup, place some sauce. Top with meringue and add more sauce over meringue.

No-Bake Icebox Cheese Cake

1½ lbs. cream cheese
¼ cup lemon juice
6 egg yolks
1 envelope plain gelatin
¾ cup hot water
6 egg whites
3 oz. sugar
1 lemon whole rind, grated
1 cup unsweetened whipped cream

1. Mix cream cheese, lemon juice, and yolks smoothly in the order given above. Scrape sides and bottom of the bowl well to avoid lumps. Dissolve the gelatin in the hot water, then add to the cheese mixture.

2. Beat the 6 egg whites with the sugar and the lemon rind until the whites are stiff but not dry. Fold the beaten egg whites into the cheese mixture.

3. Fold in the whipped cream and blend well. Pour into prepared molds, and let set for 1 hour in refrigerator.

Graham-cracker crust:

1 lb. graham crackers
6 oz. sugar
6 oz. melted sweet butter

Crush graham crackers and mix together with sugar and melted sweet butter. Press firmly on the bottom of a well-buttered 9-inch springform pan. Bake at 375° F until browned (5 minutes)

YIELD: 6 TO 8 SERVINGS

A toast to a memorable clambake. From left, Pierre Franey, Jacques Pépin, Roger Fessaquet, me and Réne Verdon.

VI

THE WEEKEND FEASTS WITH CHEFS & FRIENDS

Of the many things I cherish about my chosen trade, it is the strong and lasting friendships I have made with other chefs and people in the food industry that I value most. I have distinct and warm memories of weekends spent in Craig Claiborne's kitchen in East Hampton preparing meals with my close friends Pierre Franey, Jacques Pépin, Roger Fessaquet, René Verdon, Ed Giobbi and others—"the gang" as we used to call ourselves.

My relationships with Craig and Pierre go back many years. I first met Craig at about the time he began as food editor for the New York *Times* and I was the chef at The Colony. Pierre was really one of the first chefs I came to befriend. In fact, the day I arrived here in America to work at the Waldorf-Astoria, I was taken to lunch at Le Pavillon, at which Pierre was the chef. We were introduced to one another and right away felt a mutual kinship. It is now some thirty-seven years that Pierre and I have been together through some really great times.

Craig was the initiator of some of the best parties, picnics and feasts I have ever attended and cooked for. The parties started out small. I remember that the first such gathering took place on New Year's Eve, sometime in the late 1950s. I was still chef at The

Colony, and Pierre chef at Le Pavillon, and we had both been invited
to Craig's Greenwich Village apartment for a New Year's Eve party.
Eventually the New Year's Eve party became something of a tradition.
When it began to outgrow Craig's place in the Village, Craig bought
a house out in Clearwater, near East Hampton. He installed a
magnificent professional kitchen, the kind most chefs dream of
having in their home. By the mid-1960s the New Year's Eve parties
were published events. I vividly remember leaving for Clearwater on
Friday nights with my family and driving out to Craig's beachfront
home. There, I would meet up with Pierre, Jacques Pépin, Roger
Fessaguet, René Verdon, and, of course, Craig. We would sit around
and begin to discuss what we would prepare for the following night's
dinner.

On Saturday morning the six of us would rise early and gather
in Craig's kitchen to begin the preparations for the big event. The
noise began almost immediately as pots and pans were shifted about,
produce was chopped on the cutting board, and laughter and conversation swirled through the room. At the center of all of this excitement would be Craig, sitting at one end of the counter with pad and
pen in hand, staring through his spectacles and asking each of us
question after question about what we were making—the ingredients
involved, the procedure and so on. He would sit for hours, taking
meticulous notes that would later form the grist of his articles and
books.

What was so great about those times was the pleasure we all felt
in preparing such spectacular meals. We were an all-star team of
chefs. Pierre had been the chef at Le Pavillon, Jacques had been the
chef for Charles de Gaulle, Roger was the chef of Le Caravelle and
René was the White House chef. With all of this talent one might
expect some sort of rivalry among us. On the contrary, we all enjoyed
working with one another and did whatever had to be done, from
peeling and cleaning the vegetables to descaling the fish. The
atmosphere was both fun and relaxing. In fact, one notion that was
playfully bandied about was the idea of all of us going into a
partnership and opening a place together. This, of course, never
happened, but the point I am trying to make is that we were, above
all, friends working together to produce what would be a number of
memorable meals.

By around nine or ten o'clock in the evening the meal was ready to be enjoyed. These parties were always attended by friends of Craig, including well-known figures from the culinary, art, publishing and entertainment worlds. I remember serving such people as designer Donald Brooks; Alex Lichine, a wine importer; Sam Aaron, a wine distributor; Mervyn and Warner Le Roy; and cookbook writer Marcella Hazan, to name a few. We would all sit together around the massive dining-room table that stretched across the room and eat and drink until the early hours of the morning.

I remember one Saturday evening party when Pierre, Jacques, Roger and René set out to get me drunk on Craig's infamous Margaritas. I rarely drink to excess and my cohorts knew this full well. Anyway, I was preparing couscous for the meal and the kitchen was so hot that I felt a constant thirst. Pierre would generously offer me another drink, and yet another. By mealtime I had had numerous Margaritas and could feel their not-so-subtle effect. It was just my luck that I was seated next to a rather pompous lady. We started to make conversation, and she soon asked me in a stuffy accent, "Do you like Baaaaaach?" I looked at her and replied, 'I'm sorry, what did you say?" Again, she asked me, "Do you like Baaaaaach?" I looked over to my wife Pauline and asked her in French, "What is this lady saying?" Pauline said, "You know, Jean, Bach of classical music." By this time the Margaritas had taken their toll and I began to laugh uncontrollably. I excused myself from the table and headed for Craig's pool, where I doused my head to relieve myself of the alcohol. I remember thinking that I would have liked to have said to the lady, "No, I prefer to listen to Louis Armstrong, Sidney Bechet and Duke Ellington." They were my musical idols.

An extension of the New Year's Eve parties was the now-famous Gardiners Island Clam Bake picnic of 1965. Once again, Pierre, Jacques, Roger, René and I got together at Craig's request to produce one of the most talked-about and publicized picnics ever assembled. With all the necessary supplies on board, including dozens of Baccarat glasses, a Char-Broil grill, two cases of wine, ten crates of food and about thirty guests and friends including Howard Johnson Sr., Margaret Truman Daniel, Alfred Knopf and Mr. and Mrs. Gardiner, we shipped out to the island to begin the feast. Within minutes of landing we collected driftwood and tree trunks, and created a semi-dining area. Soon thereafter, a pit was made and a fire was built to grill the seafood and poultry. With French music filling the air, the wine bottles were opened and the feast was underway.

The menu was not your ordinary picnic menu. Each of us had prepared one aspect of it from appetizer to dessert. René prepared the pâte, Pierre made the seviche and the poached striped bass, and I prepared the grilled squab. Roger made the lobster *farci,* and Jacques satisfied the sweet tooths with his *fruits mélanges*. We wined, dined, danced and sang until the early evening. Of all the parties I have ever attended with "the gang," this is the one that remains foremost in my mind. It was, as we say, a real French "pique-nique."

There were countless other gatherings by Craig over the years that followed the Clam Bake. There was the wedding of Pierre's daughter, Claudia, held at Craig's house, which found its way into *House & Garden* magazine. And there was also the memorable party thrown by Warner Le Roy at his estate in celebration of Craig's twenty-fifth anniversary with the *Times*. Over 350 guests came, including such celebrities as Joseph Heller, Kurt Vonnegut Jr., Danny Kaye, William Styron, Walter Cronkite and many others. I and the many other chefs on hand were quite proud to be there and to have these guests sample the dishes we had created. It was our way of honoring Craig and saying thank-you for all he had given us over the twenty-five years of his stewardship at the *Times*.

I know of few food critics who have done more to promote food in this country than Craig, be it French, Italian, Chinese or Japanese. Chefs like myself came to respect him for this achievement. Unlike many critics today, he associated himself with us and came to know us as real friends. But at the same time he was not afraid to let you know when something you prepared was not as good as he felt it could be. In my business, as with any business that concerns itself with public acceptance, a partnership must exist between the critic and the chef that is based on an appreciation and acceptance of each other's work. If these elements aren't present from the start, a level of mutual respect can never, and will never, be attained. There is always value in someone else's opinion.

Another fun event that comes to mind was the time Craig invited

Before any of us could enjoy the meals there was always the preparation that needed to be done first. This included hand-picking fresh mussels (above), and chopping and cleaning our produce (below).

Pierre's family, Sirio Maccioni's and mine to spend our Memorial Day weekend in Nova Scotia, where we would prepare a meal that Craig wished to write about for the *Times*. We were to be the guests of Baron Amato, who owned a magnificent estate on the island. What I will never forget about the weekend is the boar hunt I went on with Pierre. The count happened to own a hundred-acre preserve on which over two hundred wild boar were living. So, before anyone could eat anything, Pierre and I had to hunt down and kill one of these three hundred-pound beasts—not the easiest task, since boars are notoriously dangerous and have been known to kill human beings. Though Pierre and I had been hunting numerous times before, for deer, pheasant, quail, rabbit and even bear, this was something we were really looking forward to.

We set out in early morning to find the animal. By late morning, we had spotted a herd of boars and began tracking them. We were trying to get close enough to kill one but all the while staying downwind from them so they could not smell us. At one point, Pierre indicated to me that he was in a good position to take a shot. We were only interested in killing one of the males, since there was always a chance a female might be pregnant. Pierre had spotted a male and told me it was in his sight. Just then, the grunting of the boars could be heard. The wind had apparently shifted and the boars had caught our scent. In what seemed like a split second, the entire herd was charging after us. Pierre and I began to run faster than we ever had in our lives and it was at this point that I wished I was about fifty pounds lighter. When I realized the animals were about to close in on us I yelled to Pierre to climb up the nearest tree. We both managed to avoid the herd, which ran past us. As we stared down from our perch on one of the limbs, my only thought, which I conveyed to Pierre, was what sitting ducks we would have been had we been in an open field. Shortly thereafter, we managed to bring down a nice-sized boar, which we carried back to the house. That night we roasted the boar on an open spit and embroidered the tale of our "brush with death."

Though recent years have brought less and less of these kind of events and gatherings, thinking about them still brings great joy to me. Some may wonder why we chefs would want to be doing *any* cooking at all on the weekends, when we had been doing just that throughout the week. I think my colleagues would agree with me when I say that our culinary trade has always meant more to us than just a job. As a culinary artist, I have always believed that if someone asks you to demonstrate your art for a group of people, you should be honored to have been asked. I was never paid cash for the events I participated in. Rather, I was paid in a different currency, for I was able to watch the expressions of contented people as they sampled my creations and to know that I had contributed to their pleasure.

APPETIZERS

Billi-Bi

SOUP WITH MUSSELS AND CREAM

3 lbs. mussels
2 shallots, finely chopped
1 medium onion, sliced
1 stalk parsley
  Salt and freshly ground black pepper to taste
2 cups dry white wine
3 tablespoons butter
1 small bay leaf
¼ teaspoon thyme
3 cups heavy cream
4 slightly beaten egg yolks
3 drops Tabasco

1. Scrub the mussels very well, until all the "beards" attached to the mussels have been cleaned off. Place them in a large stainless steel pot with the shallots, onions, parsley, salt, pepper, white wine, butter, bay leaf, and thyme. Cover and bring to a boil. Simmer for about 5 minutes or until mussels have opened. Discard any mussels that do not open.

2. Strain the broth through a fine sieve. Remove the mussels from the shells. Use some mussels as a garnish for the soup, and keep the leftover to be used in a cold salad.

3. Bring the broth in the saucepan to a boil. Add the cream. Return to a boil and remove from the heat. Add the beaten egg yolks and return to the heat long enough for the soup to thicken, but do not boil. Add Tabasco. Can be served hot or cold.

SERVES 6

New England Clam Chowder

2 dozen medium-size cherrystone clams
2 cups cold water
   Pinch of dried thyme
1/4 bay leaf
   2 oz. lean slab bacon, in 1/4-in. dice
   1 medium onion, chopped very fine
   1 tablespoon chopped leeks
   2 medium potatoes, peeled and diced
      Salt and freshly ground black pepper to taste
   1 cup milk
1/2 cup heavy cream (or light cream)
   1 tablespoon butter

1. Wash the clams thoroughly. Place them in a saucepan with the cold water, thyme, and bay leaf. Bring to a boil and cook slowly for 5 to 6 minutes, or until shells open.

2. Strain the clam broth through a very fine sieve. Remove the clams from their shells; clean and chop coarsely.

3. Sauté the bacon in a saucepan. Add onions and leeks. Cook slowly for about 2 minutes. Add the clams and clam broth.

4. Add the potatoes. Season with salt and black pepper and cook until potatoes are tender. On the side, bring the milk and cream to a near-boil.

5. Remove the mixture from the heat and add the milk, cream, and butter. Serve hot.

SERVES 4

Gazpacho

4 *peeled onions*
8 *peeled cucumbers*
6 *green peppers*
1 *stalk celery*
1 *bunch watercress*
15 *peeled and seeded medium-size tomatoes*
1 *bunch scallions*
1 *bunch chives*
   Juice of 4 whole limes
2 *large cloves garlic*
   Salt and white pepper to taste
¼ *cup olive oil*
¼ *cup vinegar*
1 *tablespoon Worcestershire sauce*
   Dash of Tabasco

1. Process all the vegetables and the garlic in a food processor or blender so that the ingredients stay chunky.

2. Mix in some salt, white pepper, olive oil, vinegar, Worcestershire sauce, and Tabasco and lime juice. If the soup is too thick add some tomato juice.

3. Serve the gazpacho in chilled bowls.

SERVES 6 TO 8

NOTE: Croutons, diced cucumbers, diced green pepper with chopped parsley is an excellent garnish.

Cucumber Salad

4 *large cucumbers*
1 *tablespoon salt*
3 *tablespoons red wine vinegar*

½ teaspoon freshly ground pepper
2 tablespoons vegetable oil
1 teaspoon sugar (optional)
2 tablespoons fresh chopped dill

1. Wash the cucumbers and dry them. Score the cucumbers lengthwise with a fork and slice them very thinly. Put the cucumbers in a bowl with salt, and let them rest at room temperature for a couple of hours.

2. Drain the cucumbers of all their liquid and press them in a clean towel. In a bowl beat together the vinegar, pepper, oil, sugar, and dill. Pour over the cucumbers and mix well. Keep chilled and serve cold.

SERVES 8

Guacamole

2 ripe avocados
Juice of 1 lemon
1 mashed garlic clove
4 tomatoes, peeled, seeded and coarsely chopped
½ large onion, finely chopped
¼ cup chopped celery
2 tablespoons minced parsley
¼ cup olive oil
Salt and freshly ground black pepper to taste

1. Peel and mash avocados lightly with a wooden spoon.

2. Add the lemon juice, mashed garlic, chopped tomatoes, onions, and celery and mix thoroughly.

3. Stir in the parsley, olive oil, salt and pepper.

NOTE: Leave the avocado pits in mixture until ready to serve. This will keep the Guacamole from turning brown. Serve with tostados (deep fried triangles of tortillas).

PASTAS

Pasta with Mussels

1 lb. pasta
3 lbs. mussels soaked, scrubbed, and debearded
½ cup dry white wine
1 bay leaf
2 shallots, finely chopped
3 tablespoons butter
3 cloves garlic, finely chopped
3 teaspoons chopped Italian parsley
2 cups heavy cream
   Salt and freshly ground black pepper to taste

1. Place mussels in a large saucepan with the dry white wine and bay leaf. Cook for 2 to 3 minutes or until the shells have completely opened. Remove the mussels and put them aside on a platter to cool. Strain the liquid and reserve.

2. When the mussels have cooled, remove the shells and discard them. Keep the mussels in a bowl covered with aluminum foil.

3. In a medium-size saucepan, sauté the shallots in butter until tender, add the garlic and let simmer for 1 minute. Add the reserved mussel broth, parsley, and heavy cream and let reduce by half. Then add mussels and season to taste. Pour over desired pasta and serve immediately.

SERVES 4 TO 6

Linguini with Shrimp

1 *lb. pasta*
½ *cup olive oil*
3 *cloves garlic, finely chopped*
4 *large fresh tomatoes, cut in medium-size cubes*
¼ *teaspoon of oregano*
½ *cup chopped Italian parsley*
½ *cup chopped fresh basil*
   Salt and freshly ground pepper to taste
1¼ *lbs. medium shrimp, shelled, deveined, rinsed, and*
      dried
⅓ *cup pine nuts*

1. In a saucepan heat ¼ cup of olive oil. Sauté the garlic for about 15 seconds, and add the tomatoes, oregano, parsley, basil, salt, and pepper. Let this simmer for about 2 minutes and put aside.

2. In a skillet, sauté the shrimp and pine nuts for a few minutes in the remaining olive oil. (do not overcook the shrimp)

3. Add the shrimp to the sauce and pour over the pasta.

SERVES 4 TO 6

NOTE: You can add fresh broccoli cooked al dente, if desired.

ENTRÉES

Couscous Marocain

2 lbs. lamb shoulder, cut into 1½-in. cubes
1 3-lb. cooking chicken, cut into 12 pieces
4 tablespoons olive oil
3 cups diced onions
4 quarts water
½ teaspoon saffron
½ teaspoon curry
½ teaspoon paprika
½ teaspoon cumin
½ teaspoon cinnamon
2 large cloves garlic, finely chopped
1 bay leaf
½ teaspoon thyme
¾ cup raisins
6 carrots, sliced
3 medium white turnips, diced
2 cups zucchini
2 cups diced yellow (winter) squash
2 cups diced green pepper
2 whole hot red peppers
2 cups diced celery
3 cups tomatoes, peeled and quartered
1 16-oz. can chick peas, drained and rinsed
2 lbs. medium-grained precooked couscous
3 tablespoons butter
Salt to taste

1. Place oil, meat, and chicken in the bottom of a couscoussière. Cook on top of the range at a medium heat. Add the onions and sauté, stirring, for 5 to 6 minutes without browning. Add 1 quart water, the spices, and cover. Bring to a boil then let simmer for 1 to 1½ hours.

2. Add the raisins, carrots, turnips, zucchini, yellow squash, green pepper, hot peppers, celery, tomatoes, and chick peas. Return to a boil and simmer for 30 minutes, skimming the fat.

3. Pour couscous into a mixing bowl and pour in 3 quarts boiling water. Add salt to taste, stir and let sit for 2 to 3 minutes. Place couscous in top section of the couscoussiere, then put it on top of the base part in order to steam it for 5 minutes and absorb flavors from below. Be sure the couscous does not touch the liquid. Stir occasionally with a fork.

4. Add butter and fluff couscous with a fork. Arrange couscous in a ring on a large platter leaving the middle empty. Place the stew in the middle of the platter.

SERVES 10 TO 12

NOTE: The couscous can be accompanied with a hot sauce (see page 179), and a bowl of bouillon on the side.

Grilled Squabs

½ cup dry mustard
⅓ cup dry white wine
　Salt and freshly ground black pepper to taste
15 squabs, split for broiling
　Peanut oil
1 quart fresh bread crumbs

1. Combine the mustard, wine, and salt in a mixing bowl. Let stand.

2. Prepare a charcoal fire. The bed of coals should be about 1 foot from the grilling surface. When the coals are hot and have a white ash, prepare the squabs.

3. Brush the squabs with oil and sprinkle with salt and pepper. Place squabs, skin side down, on the grill and cook 8 minutes.

4. Turn squabs and brush again with oil, salt and pepper. Grill 8 minutes, then brush on both sides with the mustard paste.

5. Have the bread crumbs ready in a flat pan and dip the squabs into the bread crumbs on both sides to coat them well. Sprinkle with more oil and continue grilling on both sides. Total cooking time is about 25 minutes.

SERVES 30

Poulet Sauté Chasseur
CHICKEN SAUTÉ HUNTER STYLE

3 chickens, 2½ lbs. each
6 tablespoons butter
1 tablespoon finely chopped onions
1 tablespoon finely chopped shallots
1 bay leaf
　Pinch of thyme

½ *cup dry white wine*
3 *cups chicken broth or beef broth*
3 *cups diced fresh tomatoes or 3 cups canned*
tomatoes
½ *lb. fresh mushrooms, sliced*
Salt and freshly ground pepper to taste
1 *tablespoon flour*
1 *teaspoon chopped fresh tarragon, or ½ teaspoon*
dried
Chopped parsley

1. Cut chicken into pieces, and put 4 tablespoons butter into a large, deep frying pan. Melt the butter and when hot, place the chicken into the pan and sauté until it is golden brown on all sides. Then add the chopped onions, shallots, bay leaf, and thyme, and cook for 3 to 4 minutes.

2. Add the wine, broth, tomatoes, mushrooms, salt, and pepper. Cook slowly for another 15 to 20 minutes.

3. Take the chicken pieces out of the sauce and keep warm in the oven.

4. Boil the sauce slowly and thicken it with 2 tablespoons of butter blended with 1 tablespoon of flour. Add the tarragon and let boil slowly for 3 minutes.

5. Pour the sauce over the chicken pieces and simmer for 2 minutes. Before serving, sprinkle the chopped parsley on top.

SERVES 6

Southern Fried Chicken

1 2½-lb. chicken, cut into serving pieces
Milk
Tabasco
1 tablespoon or more freshly ground black pepper
1 lb. lard
¼ lb. butter
    Flour for dredging
    Salt to taste

1. Place the chicken parts in a mixing bowl and add milk to cover. Add a few drops of Tabasco and about ½ teaspoon black pepper. Let stand an hour or refrigerate overnight.

2. When ready to cook, begin melting the lard and butter in a large heavy skillet. (Butter and lard can be replaced by vegetable oil.)

3. Drain the milk off but do not dry the chicken. Place in a large bowl with enough flour to coat the chicken; add salt to taste and the remaining black pepper. Dredge the chicken parts in the flour.

4. While the lard and butter are still melting, begin to add the chicken pieces, skin side down. Turn the heat to high and cook the chicken until it becomes brown, then turn the pieces, using tongs. Turn the heat down to moderately low and continue cooking the chicken pieces until golden brown. Continue cooking until the meat is thoroughly cooked. 20 minutes or longer. Drain well on paper towels before serving.

SERVES 2

Côtes de Marcassin
WILD BOAR CHOPS WITH MUSTARD SAUCE

8–10 wild boar or pork chops, cut ½ in. thick
Salt and freshly ground pepper to taste
Flour for dredging
5 tablespoons butter
½ tablespoon finely chopped shallots
½ tablespoon finely chopped onion
½ cup dry white wine
2 tablespoons red wine vinegar
1 tablespoon imported Dijon mustard
3 tablespoons thinly sliced cornichons (imported small
French sour pickles) or small sour pickles
2 tablespoons finely chopped parsley.

1. Sprinkle the chops on all sides with salt and pepper. Coat lightly on all sides with flour and shake off excess.

2. Heat 3 tablespoons of butter in a large heavy skillet. Add the chops and brown on one side. Turn and brown on the other side, turning often, about 15 to 20 minutes. Transfer the chops to a heated platter and keep warm.

3. Add the shallots and onion to the skillet and when wilted and starting to brown, add the wine, stirring. Add the red wine vinegar and reduce briefly. Stir in the mustard. Add the cornichons. Heat briefly and add the remaining 2 tablespoons of butter, bit by bit, swirling it in. Pour this over the chops and sprinkle with chopped parsley.

SERVES 4 TO 5

Grilled Marinated Lamb Chops

6 lamb chops
Salt and freshly ground pepper to taste
½ cup lemon juice
½ cup olive oil or corn oil
½ cup finely chopped mint
2 teaspoons grated lemon rind
1 clove garlic, finely chopped

1. Sprinkle the chops with salt and pepper on both sides.

2. Combine remaining ingredients in a small bowl and blend well.

3. Place the lamb chops in a flat dish, just large enough to hold them, and pour marinade mixture over them. Marinate chops 2 to 4 hours, turning them occasionally.

4. When ready to serve, broil over charcoal for 5 minutes, turn and broil 5 minutes longer, or until chops are cooked through. Brush chops with marinade mixture during cooking time.

SERVES 3 TO 4

Moules Marseillaise
MUSSELS MARSEILLAISE

2 tablespoons butter
2 tablespoons olive oil
1 tablespoon finely chopped shallots
2 tablespoons finely chopped onions
1 teaspoon finely chopped garlic
½ cup seeded and finely chopped sweet red pepper
1½ cups skinned, seeded, and chopped tomatoes
Freshly ground black pepper to taste
Pinch of cayenne
6 lbs. mussels, scrubbed and cleaned
1 cup dry white wine

½ teaspoon saffron
2 tablespoons butter
　Salt and pepper if necessary
2 tablespoons fresh chopped parsley

1. In a large pot, heat the butter and oil, then add the shallots, onion, and garlic, and sauté for 1 minute. Add the sweet red pepper and sauté for 1 more minute. Now add the tomatoes, ground pepper, and cayenne and sauté 2 more minutes.

2. Add the white wine and mussels. Cover and allow to boil for 2 to 3 minutes or until the shells are open. Lift the mussels from the broth, place them in a deep casserole dish, cover them, and set aside, keeping them warm.

3. Add the saffron to the broth already prepared and reduce by half at moderate heat. Correct seasoning.

4. Thicken the sauce with the butter over a medium heat, adding the butter bit by bit to the hot broth. Mix with a wire whisk until the butter has melted into the broth. Pour over the mussels and sprinkle with chopped parsley.

SERVES 6

Paella

¾ lb. chorizo or hot Italian sausage
1 2-lb. lobster
½ cup olive oil
1 3-lb. chicken, cut in 8 pieces
  Salt and freshly ground pepper to taste
16 medium shrimp, shelled, deveined, and rinsed
1 cup diced smoked ham
1 cup chopped onion
4 cloves garlic, finely chopped
3 large sweet pimientos, cut in strips
16 pitted green olives
3 large tomatoes, diced
½ teaspoon saffron
2 cups rice, cooked
1 chili pepper
2 cups chicken broth
16 large mussels
8 medium-size clams
1 cup frozen peas, cooked
1 tablespoon chopped parsley

1. Preheat oven to 375° F.

2. Pierce the sausage with a fork and blanch in boiling water for 2 minutes, cool and slice into ½-in. pieces.

3. Cut the claws and legs off the lobster, remove the tail, and slice the body into 1-in. pieces. Remove and discard the small sack inside the lobster, near the eyes.

4. Heat ½ cup of olive oil in a Paella pan or in a large skillet. Sprinkle the chicken with salt and pepper, Sauté chicken, stirring the pieces around the pan until browned, about 3 to 4 minutes. Remove to a platter.

5. Sprinkle the shrimp with salt and pepper and sauté them very quickly for about 1 minute, be sure not to overcook, and remove.

6. Sauté the pieces of sausage for 1 minute, remove to the platter, and discard the fat in the skillet.

7. Heat remaining ¼ cup olive oil in pan and sauté diced ham for one minute and remove to platter. Add the onion, garlic, red sweet pimentos, olives, tomatoes, and saffron. Cook for about 5 minutes, stirring constantly.

8. Add the cooked rice with the onion and tomato mixture, mixing thoroughly, then add the chili peppers. Bring the chicken broth to a boil and then pour it into the rice mixture. Place the mussels and clams into the oven for 25 minutes. Serve the rice with all the sautéd ingredients, mussels, clams, cooked peas, and parsley on top. Serve very hot.

SERVES 6 TO 8

Irish Stew

6 lbs. lamb shoulder, cut in 1-in. cubes
4 tablespoons butter
3 leeks, coarsely chopped
3 large onions, coarsley chopped
1 lb. cabbage, coarsely chopped
2 cloves garlic
1 bouquet garni (parlsey, 2 bay leafs, and ½
    teaspoon dried thyme tied together in
    cheesecloth)
  Salt and freshly ground pepper to taste
2 lbs. small white onions
3 lbs. potatoes peeled and cut into balls with a melon
    scoop
  Worcestershire sauce to taste

1. Place lamb in a deep kettle and cover with cold water. Bring to a boil for 2 to 3 minutes. Drain off the hot water. Set the meat aside.

2. Clean the kettle. Melt butter, and toss the leeks, onions, cabbage, garlic, and bouquet garni for 2 to 3 minutes. Add the lamb, salt, pepper, and enough water to cover. Bring to a boil. Let it cook for another 30 minutes until the meat is tender.

3. In another pan, cook the small onions in boiling water until tender. Add potato balls to salted boiling water and cook until tender.

4. Remove the lamb with a slotted spoon. Keep warm on the side. Drain the liquid from the vegetables that were cooked with the lamb and also set aside. Purée the vegetables and gradually add the liquid until the desired consistency of a thick soup is attained.

5. Return the meat and purée to the kettle. Add the onions and potato balls and simmer for 5 to 6 minutes. Correct the seasoning and add Worcestershire sauce to taste.

SERVES 12

Chili con Carne

2 lbs. red kidney beans
4 large onions
2 cloves
2 green peppers
3 tablespoons butter
3 tablespoons oil
4–5 garlic cloves, finely chopped
5 lbs. ground beef
1 lb. ground pork
4 tablespoons chili powder
1 35-oz. can Italian plum tomatoes
2 7-ounce cans tomato paste
1 tablespoon salt
1½ teaspoons freshly ground black pepper
2 teaspoons oregano
2 teaspoons ground cumin
2 bay leaves
½ teaspoon Tabasco
½ cup chopped parsley
3–4 cups beef stock

1. Put the red kidney beans in a bowl and cover with boiling water. Let the beans soak overnight.

2. The next day, cook the beans in the soaking liquid with one large onion stuck with 2 cloves. When cooked, drain, reserving the liquid.

3. Chop the remaining onions, and seed and chop the green peppers. Sauté these ingredients in the butter and oil until golden brown.

4. Add the garlic, cook for 2 minutes, and then add the ground beef and ground pork. Cook the meat, breaking it up with a fork or wooden spoon until browned.

5. Stir in the chili powder and cook for 5 minutes. Then add the Italian plum tomatoes, tomato paste, salt, black pepper, oregano, cumin, bay leaves, Tabasco, parsley, and enough beef stock to cover the meat.

6. Simmer for 2½ hours, taste and correct the seasoning, then mix in the beans and bring to a boil. If the chili is too thick, add a little of the bean liquid to give the desired consistency. Serve hot.

SERVES 10 TO 12

SAUCES

Hot Sauce

  2 hot red chili peppers
  ½ cup olive oil
    Few drops Tabasco
  ½ cup hot water
  · Dash cayenne
    Black pepper to taste
  ½ teaspoon coriander

Mix all the ingredients in a blender or food processor.

YIELDS 1 CUP

Aioli for Boiled or Steamed Vegetables & Fish
GARLIC MAYONNAISE

  3 egg yolks
  5 cloves garlic, finely chopped
    Juice of ½ lemon
    Salt and freshly ground black pepper to taste
    Dash of cayenne
    Drop of Tabasco
  2 cups olive oil
  1 medium baked potato (keep only the pulp; discard
    the skin)

1. Place the yolks in a mixing bowl. Add garlic, lemon juice, salt, pepper, cayenne, and Tabasco.

2. Beat with a wire whisk, gradually adding the oil. When the mixture starts to thicken add the potato pulp. Continue beating until all the oil has been used. If the mixture is too thick, add a few drops of water.

YIELDS 2½ CUPS

Gathered around Sirio and me is Le Cirque's fine crew.

VII

AT LE CIRQUE RESTAURANT

I believe that as long as man is on this earth, and has pennies in his pocket, he will try to find a place to feed and entertain himself. Food is clearly the basis of survival, but the notion that it can be so much more than that is what finally made the risk of opening Le Cirque worth taking. To be sure, there were the economic realities and other hurdles that inevitably lie in the path of any new business venture. But it was the simple joy of sharing my love for cuisine with a world of equally enthusiastic people that became my own driving force.

As early as 1971, three years prior to the actual opening of Le Cirque, Sirio was in contact with me by telephone to tell me he was scouting out possibilities. By this time I had left Stop & Shop, Inc., and was working in New Hampshire at a place called the Brick Yard Mountain Inn. I was involved in trying to help open a small restaurant there that was to be part of the inn itself. I must admit this was not one of my better business decisions. The restaurant never came into being because of lack of financing, and I found the pace of life in New Hampshire to be overly slow for my personality. I still had a lot of drive and ambition to succeed, and I felt I was too far away from the New York scene. I really wanted to get back into the thick of things.

At about the same time that I was growing weary of New Hampshire, Pierre Franey had been asked by Warner Le Roy—the owner of Maxwell's Plum—if he knew of anyone who could fill the position of executive chef at his restaurant. Pierre told him that he had just the man. Soon thereafter, at one of the many East Hampton parties, I met Warner and he offered me the position. I can recall him saying, "Jean, what is a chef like you doing way up there in New Hampshire? You must come back to New York where you belong and work for me at Maxwell's Plum." He made me an offer I couldn't refuse. Once again, my family had to pack their bags and make the move to New Jersey, where we decided to live. I don't think the move bothered my wife too much, but my sons Robert and Roger were reluctant to leave. They both loved to ski in the winters, and New Hampshire not only provided them with this opportunity but with a lot more. For them, the thought of moving to New Jersey and making new friends was less than appealing. When I was a young man I had moved about extensively, working in Denmark, the south of France, Paris, the Alps and Bermuda, but I never really thought twice about my itinerancy because it was necessary to learn my trade. Now, though, with a family to worry about, there were bigger stakes involved. Not only my life, but my wife's and children's as well, would be affected by my decision. Despite this, I knew that coming back to New York was the right move for all of us. I would have been even more certain in that conviction had I known the decision would lead, eventually, to opening Le Cirque with Sirio.

Maxwell's Plum was quite different from any place I had ever worked before. The menu was designed so that anyone who wanted to eat could find something among the choices that they liked. For example, the menu carried Warner's favorite—the Maxwell's Plum hamburger, which boasted itself to be the biggest in New York. Also on the menu were such dishes as chili con carne, escargot, pepper steak, chef's salads and a whole range of fish, soups, pastas and desserts. The menu appealed to eccentric and diverse tastes, as did the dining room's decor. If you have never been to Maxwell's Plum you must pay a visit simply to gaze at the interior, which is filled with porcelain animals, mosaic glass, waterfalls and countless other ornate fixtures—all designed by Warner to give the customers the feeling of casual dining in a relaxed yet opulent atmosphere. It resembled a fabulous palace. It also had a more formal dining area with an à la carte menu for those customers who wished to dine in more luxury. With two kinds of dining rooms, it provided for a mixture of people, from the tourist who happened to drop in off the street to the uppercrust lady and gentleman of New York who knew Warner or knew of him and came to eat in his "palace," as he himself called it.

Because of—perhaps in spite of—its attempt to appeal to everyone, Maxwell's Plum was a fine restaurant. We had a three-star rating from the *Times* while I was there. For me, the menu provided a chance to experiment with various spices and foods, since the selections extended beyond the strict classic cuisine I had served at The Colony. The volume of buying was also much greater than at The Colony because the menu was so diverse. It was a good place for me to return to, after New Hampshire, drawing me back into the hustle and bustle that distinguishes New York's restaurant life. It was here that I met Jean Louis Todeschini, who was the sous chef at Maxwell's Plum. When I left Maxwell's to open Le Cirque I would bring Jean Louis with me and install him as chef. He was a young and brilliant chef who demonstrated the creativity and imagination I knew I would need at Le Cirque.

In my opinion, and I am sure that I speak for many others, Warner has shown himself to be a genius in creating places as successful as Maxwell's Plum, Tavern on the Green, and most recently his new restaurant in Washington, D.C. As a restauranteur he realizes that most people these days prefer to dine in a casual setting and enjoy themselves through the ambience a place has to offer. I know of few places that offer the same casual, yet exciting, ambience that Maxwell's Plum and Tavern on the Green do.

It was while working at Maxwell's Plum—the year was 1972— that I was again contacted by Sirio, who was working at Le Fôret at the Pierre Hotel. He told me that William Zeckendorf Jr., the real-estate magnate, had contacted him about opening a small, elegant, upper-scale restaurant in the old Mayfair Hotel on East Sixty-fifth Street, which William was renovating.

Wishing to recapture some of the "good old days" of The Colony, William wanted both Sirio and me to be proprietors of this venture. He knew we could be a great team, with Sirio controlling the dining room, and me the kitchen, as it had been at The Colony. Yet we were apprehensive. Although Sirio and I knew what it took to satisfy customers, it didn't take a genius to see that in 1972 the restaurant business in New York was taking a real beating due to the economic problems that plagued the city as well as the rest of the country.

At that point we sat down and took stock. We knew we had the right game plan and the ingredients to make it work—initiative, self-confidence and the trust in one another as partners that is so essential in taking such a risk. In the end, we decided we'd be kicking ourselves ever afterward if we didn't seize the opportunity. So, Sirio and I met with William to discuss all the details that were involved in opening the restaurant. The first decision to make was what to name the place. At first I wanted to call it Le Dauphiné, the name for the province I come from in France. To my chagrin we learned that another restaurant had this name. I then suggested Le Dauphinois, which was the name for a person who came from the Dauphine province of France. Unfortunately, we learned that this name, too, was already being used by another restaurant. Then one day the three of us were with some friends of William's who had just returned from Paris. They told us they had been to a Paris club called Le Cirque. When we heard the name, William, Sirio and I looked at each other; it was perfect. The name would be Le Cirque, which in French has two connotations: the more familiar one, "circus," and also "a group of people who get together to have a good time."

The next decision to be made was how to design the place. Fortunately, William was a close friend of the well-known designer Ellen Lehman McCloskey. Taking her cue from the name "Le Cirque," she chose to duplicate the Singerie Room in the Palace of Versailles, which would give the dining room an elegant, almost feminine aura. We were all quite pleased with the way things were coming together. Luckily, we would be using a kitchen that had been set up when the hotel had originally been built. It was not a typical restaurant kitchen. It was much larger because it had been designed to cater to the large number of people a hotel would have. But we weren't complaining; we could always use the extra space. The dining room was the most important thing anyway, because that is what the customers would see and react to.

By March of 1974 the remodeling of the dining room was completed. A separate entrance on Sixty-fifth Street had also been built so that customers need not walk through the hotel to get to the restaurant. We wanted our own identity, separate from the hotel, and the entrance provided this. At Le Cirque's inception our aim was simply to try to recapture the same elegance and quality of cuisine that had been associated with The Colony. In fact, some critics even called us the "stepchild" of The Colony. Contrary to what one might think, the association pleased us because it attracted the same clients Sirio and I used to serve. After our opening night, it was clear to us that we had succeeded in our aim, and we felt confident that Le Cirque would have a bright future in New York.

Although success did come quickly for us, there was some criticism regarding our approach. Some New York critics felt we were located too far uptown to attract a steady lunch patronage. In the 1970s critics felt that if a restaurant could not attract the midtown crowd for lunch, it would go out of business. But I think that when the critics saw celebrities such as the late Princess Grace of Monaco, Lady Keith, the late Duchess of Windsor, Macolm Forbes, Elizabeth Taylor, Oscar de la Renta, Richard Nixon, Mikhail Baryshnikov, Frank Sinatra, Richard Burton, Henry Kissinger and Margaret Truman Daniel come for lunch and dinner, week after week, they were disabused of that notion. There were those critics who accused us of shunning the nouveaux riche and catering solely to those who had old money. I don't know what gave rise to this criticism because Sirio and I specifically set out to make sure each and every customer was treated properly. Sirio and I both realized that restauranteurs faced with increasing competition could not afford to be arrogant or to dictate to their customers. Of course, if there was a client who came to eat at Le Cirque three times a week, it only made sense that he be well taken care of. But even if we were seeing a customer for the first time, we tried our best to make sure he received equal treatment.

Though New York's food critics are, with very few exceptions, intelligent and conscientious, their opinions are often taken as fact, which over the years has caused me and other restauranteurs more than a little consternation. I often feel critics would be more charitable if they had a greater understanding of the work involved in running a place like Le Cirque. Ultimately, of course, all

*Posing with two of
France's greatest
chefs, my good
friends Paul Bocuse
(far right) and Roger
Vergé (behind me).
Also pictured are
Le Cirque chefs,
Michel Bourdeaux
(front) and Jean Louis
Todeschini (back).*

reviews—even mixed reviews—are beneficial, for, as Gene Cavallero once told me, a restaurant must achieve a certain standard to be written about in the first place. We were getting the kind of publicity that could only help our image.

Though many parallels can be drawn between Le Cirque and The Colony, there were very original aspects to Le Cirque. Though we maintained an atmosphere of elegance within our dining room, Sirio and I established an open-seating reservation. That is to say, although we took reservations we did not assign tables. We felt that every table was the best table, and wanted each client to feel as important and catered to as the next. This notion was a radical departure from what prevailed at The Colony, where every table was assigned a certain ranking. The more important the client, the better the table he received. This usually meant that if one had no social standing he was seated in what we called Siberia. I can recall Sirio telling me that when he was maître d' at The Colony, Jackie Kennedy and her sister Lee Radziwell requested his private phone number so that they would be guaranteed their special tables. At Le Cirque we wanted to change this old practice. And we did. We also decided not to have a strict dress code. Women could come in pants and men with an ascot. This was most unique for a restaurant of Le Cirque's caliber. I think that in 1974 the attitude of people in general was far less sophisticated and stuffy than it was in the 1950s. I can recall walking into the dining room of The Colony and rarely hearing a voice raised. Even when people at a table laughed, the mirth was contained. At Le Cirque, though, the crowd was far more diversified and far more able to express and enjoy themselves in public. To attract these types of people, Sirio and I did not require the regimented look of a suit and tie, or a women's long evening gown. As long as you appeared clean and proper, you were always welcome.

We also tried to create a cozier setting by bringing the tables closer together than is usual for such restaurants. We wanted to echo Le Cirque's less familiar connotation of comraderie. A unique dining-room feature was the private L'Orangerie Room. This room provided an opportunity to cater to the private parties and social functions of wealthier clients. It was rare to have such a large room to hold special occasions, and it allowed us an added feature our rivals did not have. It was literally "fireworks" in the kitchen on those nights when we had a private party in the L'Orangerie Room for 150 guests, and at the same time had reservations for another 150 to 180 in the restaurant. On such nights I had to draw on all my prior experience to make sure everything ran smoothly. Obviously, the menu for the private party was known in advance, and much of it was prepared beforehand. But still, everything had to be cooked that night. The thought of going out to the customers and saying, "I'm sorry your food was not to your liking, but we are just so busy in the kitchen—we have a private party going on," was for me totally unacceptable. I myself would find such an excuse infuriating, and so I never wanted my customers to have to hear those words.

These nights in the kitchen were particularly stressful, but I always accepted the stress as a reality of the trade. The plain truth is that customers don't want excuses. They pay for quality and they expect quality. One must be aware of this when choosing the restaurant business—indeed, any service business—as a livelihood. I can remember, after one of these exhausting nights, going to Regine's or Melon's with some of the crew and having a drink and a bite to eat, and just trying to wind down. I would not get home until the early hours of the morning, and Pauline would always wonder where I'd been.

In terms of cuisine, there were subtle differences between Le Cirque and The Colony. Although during that first year on Sixty-fifth Street I used many of the memorable recipes I'd created while at The Colony, their preparation and presentation were modified to better suit the times.

We incorporated, for example, a new style of serving on over-sized plates called *à l'assiette*. At The Colony we'd made it a practice to bring the meat out in front of the customer, where the captain would prepare and serve the dish. This old method took away many of the creative opportunities for the chef. So I began to do what my friends and fellow chefs such as Roger Vergé, Paul Bocuse, Jean Trois Gros and Alain Chapel were doing in their restaurants in France. Each order, each plate, was decorated by the chef in the kitchen. Here, the garnishes and the sauces were applied as well. This allowed the chef the opportunity to demonstrate more of his creative and artistic talents.

Another practice I adhered to was that of making the sauces more delicate. Society in the 1970s had become much more health conscious than ever before. Some found the classic French sauces burdensome, with their heavy reliance on cream and butter, so lighter sauces were created that didn't compromise the taste. This was done by first completely eliminating what is called the *roux*—a mixture of butter and flour—and then reducing the stock as well as the butter and cream.

Of course, if you are in the business of serving *real* French cuisine, which I certainly was, you still have to use the basics: butter, cream, wine, cognac and champagne. You don't always have to compromise. For example, if someone wants Eggs Benedict, it will most assuredly be made with Hollandaise Sauce, as it has been for the past two hundred years. The sauce itself is not heavy but is quite rich. So the thing to do is simply apply one spoonful of the

Hollandaise Sauce to the egg rather than two. Such was the approach we took at Le Cirque.

The brown sauce called *espagnol,* made for such dishes as veal marsala and tournedos Rossini, was changed as well. To thicken this sauce we used cornstarch, as opposed to the roux we had used in the past. The cornstarch served the same purpose and is healthier.

We also reduced the classic *vin blanc* sauce, the basic sauce for the fish. It used to be made with fish stock, white wine and a little roux. At Le Cirque we first reduced the fish stock, then added a bit of butter and cream. Though the sauce retained its richness, it was not as heavy as before. Such minor adjustments were as far as I would go in deviating from the time-honored principles of classic French cuisine. Anyone who says he or she can make good food without butter, cream, wine and liquor is grossly incorrect.

Because of my French peasant background, I felt that the addition of provincial dishes from the *campagne de France* would enhance the menu. Though we served a wealthy urbane clientele I did not feel we should be above serving such plebian dishes. Served in the traditional French style, these dishes included lamb curry, *blanquette de veau, choucroute garni, cassoulet,* and *tête de veau ravigote*. For those who preferred salad or a breast of chicken, these too were included on the menu. I have always believed that when you leave a restaurant you should feel full and satisfied. Indeed, I have the waistline to prove it. I am not a strong believer in the cuisine minceur (nouvelle cuisine), and it is not something that all chefs want to conform to (see the Epilogue, on the future of cuisine). Though my family tells me that I should be the first to embrace this cuisine, I would rather look like a well-fed man than a gentleman that can fit into a double-breasted suit.

Returning to my discussion of the differences between Le Cirque and The Colony, the size of Le Cirque's kitchen crew was also modified and slimmed down in comparison to The Colony. Because of the overhead, it was virtually impossible for any restaurant in the '70s to carry the same number of staff as had been typical in the past. Though the stations remained intact—I still kept a saucier, entremetier, poissonnier, rôtisseur, garde-manger and pastry chef—I did not have several assistants working at each station. With the times being the way they were, it was impossible for a restaurant to carry station assistants and expect to make a profit. I used to spend at least $30,000 on food alone each month, so when salaries, liquor-license payments and lease payments were factored in, the overhead was incredible. This is why I often smile when I hear people say, "Let's open a restaurant" or "Wouldn't it be great to have our own place." If they only knew what was involved. The headaches are even greater when you are dealing with a quality French restaurant, where professionalism and excellent food are mandatory.

With the changes that Sirio and I implemented, both in the dining room and with respect to the cuisine, the restaurant was able to move away from its image as "a stepchild" of The Colony and to create its own unique and much-talked-about atmosphere. One of the greatest contributors to this evolution was our version of Pasta Primavera, probably the most famous and popular dish served during my years at Le Cirque. Though it generated a great deal of publicity, few critics or gourmets knew the story behind the recipe.

To be honest, although the idea for the recipe was mine initially, I cannot take full credit for it. I have seen too many instances in which a chef will take the credit for a recipe that was really created by those who worked for him in the kitchen. I think this is very wrong! Le Cirque's Pasta Primavera recipe was a result of the combined efforts of my chef, Jean Louis Todeschini, Sirio Maccioni and me.

The idea for the dish came to me while at a dinner party at my friend's house, Ed Giobbi. Ed is not only a fine painter but has also written some excellent books on Italian cuisine. That night, Ed prepared a dish of linguini, olive oil and garlic, with fresh asparagus and other fresh vegetables from his garden. Immediately my mind started turning. I was always thinking about new recipes to add to the menu, and the idea of fresh vegetables served with pasta intrigued me.

The following day I discussed the concept with Jean Louis. I told him that I wanted to use some fresh asparagus, string beans, zucchini and mushrooms. Jean Louis suggested adding pea pods and using a bit of cream and butter to make it more French. Still, it was looking a bit too green; it needed more color. I decided to add some tomatoes. We then tried a variety of different things, experimenting to find the right amount of each vegetable for the best taste. We eventually arrived at what we felt was the right concoction: we would use zucchini, broccoli, snow peas, baby peas, asparagus and mushrooms. On the side we would sauté some fresh tomatoes. At Sirio's suggestion we added pignoli nuts and basil. Then the pasta was served with the bouquet of vegetables. It really looked quite colorful and delicious. I suggested using grated Swiss cheese instead of Parmesan, but both Sirio and Jean Louis preferred Parmesan, so Parmesan it was.

The recipe was an immediate success. At about the time we began serving the Pasta Primavera, Pierre Franey and Mimi Sheraton happened to be at Le Cirque for lunch. Both tried the dish and loved it. A few days later Craig Claiborne sampled it and was moved to write about it in *The New York Times Magazine*. *House & Garden* magazine asked Sirio and me to reproduce the recipe in their studio for yet another article. With all this publicity, the Primavera came to be requested more and more, as a main course as well as an appetizer. Ironically, the dish was never listed in the menu. Since it required an awful lot of preparation, we did not overpublicize it; the dish itself generated its own demand.

Le Cirque was truly a phenomenon, and Sirio and I were enjoying each and every minute of it. As a simple country boy whose hometown couldn't be located on a map, I was overwhelmed by the restaurant's success. Who would have believed?

I knew things were going particularly well for us when I received two special awards in conjunction with my work at Le Cirque. In 1977, the French government awarded me the Mérite Agricole. This award, given by the Minister d'Agricole, honors a person who, through his career, has pursued and promoted the French culinary tradition. Unlike Americans, the French take their culinary tradition very seriously and have an institutional apparatus set up to honor those who advance that tradition. The Mérite Agricole has much meaning for me, as it represents not only the approval and acclaim of my peers, but the approval of my home country as well.

The capstone of my career as a chef and restaurateur also came in 1978, when L' Association des Maîtres Cuisiniers de France elected me Chef of the Year, an award given to an exceptional chef who has also succeeded in establishing his own outstanding restaurant. Translated in English, the award states:

> The term *maître cuisinier* designates the chef who demonstrates authority in his art.
>
> To be recognized as maître cuisinier, a certain number of conditions must be met. First, the chef must have accomplished a serious apprenticeship, justified by a stay of exercise of the trade with an affirmed professional competence, and possess extensive knowledge relating to the activity of being a chef.
>
> The satisfaction of these conditions marks the commencement of the master.
>
> Therefore, the title of maître cuisinier is granted by a professional commission. It corresponds to an experienced technical ability—to a superior qualification in the trade and within a recognized professional culture.
>
> The listing of the maîtres cuisiniers is, therefore, not a register of selected restaurants. Rather, it is a list of men who have mastered the art of the trade, having an affirmed competence, and who exercise their art with conscience, whatever the style or degree of comfort or luxury of the establishments in which they work, in either the capacity of owner or chef de cuisine.

I think that most people, in any field, would agree that to be honored by one's peers is one of life's greatest satisfactions. During my long career as a chef and restauranteur I have had the privilege of receiving several awards for my effort in demonstrating and advancing French cuisine. Although I try to retain a basic humility, these distinctions have touched me deeply. I don't quite know how to express it in English. In French we have a saying: *fiere de toi* (proud of oneself).

There has always been a strong sense of pride inherent in the French cooking tradition; for this reason, it has always disturbed me that, in America, chefs are called cooks. This, I believe, is a slight to practitioners of the culinary art. In France, a chef is not a servant, but is as revered as a doctor, professor or, quite appropriately an artist. Perhaps, with the exposure that a number of new and promis-

Sharing the Chef of The Year Award with my two principal chefs,
Jean Louis Todeschini and Michel Bourdeaux.

ing American chefs are beginning to receive, such a careless view may soon be corrected.

I must emphasize that a chef should not be too enamored by awards. One will lose ground very quickly if he thinks he knows it all or has achieved it all. Food changes every day. Like a chemist, a chef must continually experiment—with new vegetables, spices and methods. Nobody can claim he knows everything about food. The best one can do is to learn to adapt to, or better yet, anticipate, the changes that will occur.

I must admit at this point that I have known many chefs more complete than I. But they never acquired the same recognition because they refused to accept the extended responsibilities of being a chef or owner. As a young chef I devoted most of my free time to nurturing a more socially active French culinary society here in New York. I involved myself with such clubs as the Vatel Club, Chef de Cuisine de l'America, and the Société Culinaire Philanthropique. During my years at Le Cirque I tried to help young Americans who showed a willingness to learn the trade. When the Culinary Institute of America, located in Hyde Park, asked me if I would be interested in allowing some of the apprentices the opportunity to come to Le Cirque for one-week sessions, I was always more than happy to allow these men and women the chance to see how the kitchen operated. I can think of no better training for these apprentices than to watch and participate in the preparation and execution of a lunch or dinner serving. It is gratifying for me to know that many of the young people I have helped have continued in the trade and have accomplished what they set out to do. One such young man, Kevin Collins, operates his own restaurant, Fresh Fields Café, in Chatham, New Jersey. A young woman who worked for me, Patricia Chuckac, is presently the head chef at Muhlenberg College. Another associate, Michael Gussenfeld, is the chef at the Grand Café in Morristown, New Jersey. And yet another young man, Robert Bagli, is presently the saucier at Le Chantilly Restaurant in New York. Though these four Americans most often compete in a trade dominated by Europeans, they've demonstrated the sort of ambition and willingness that America needs to legitimize its cuisine.

I've always believed that I must share my knowledge in gratitude for the opportunities my profession has afforded me. Indeed, this chance to share my knowledge has proved to be one of my greatest satisfactions.

If I have one regret about Le Cirque it is that I wish I had opened it at a younger age. I was fifty years old when it first opened. The ambition and aggressiveness that marked my early years had mellowed by that time. The heat of the kitchen and the long hours on one's feet had a way of making an old man feel even older. Even so, not for one minute do I regret shouldering, along with Sirio, the responsibility of running Le Cirque. It was, as I said very early in this book, a dream come true.

Le Cirque's success also gave me the opportunity to meet people and attend public events that I would not have otherwise. One memory that stands out in particular is the time I was invited to perform a demonstration on the *Dinah Shore Show*. Dinah had asked me if I would be willing to fly out to Hollywood, because that particular week she was doing shows on different foods of the world. I gladly accepted, with the notion that it would be great fun, as well as good publicity for Le Cirque. On arriving at the airport in Los Angeles, I saw a man in full uniform holding up a big card that had my name on it in block letters. He told me he was my chauffeur and that he was to escort me back to the Beverly Hills Hotel. Anyone who knows me will tell you that I am a very simple man and have never behaved as if I were a celebrity. So, needless to say, this treatment caught me somewhat off balance.

When we got to the street I saw a huge limousine and wondered who was in it. Perhaps I could get a glimpse of a movie star. To my disbelief my chauffeur went over to the limousine and opened the door. I couldn't believe that the car was for me. By this time, people had gathered around the car and I could hear them asking one another, "Who is this man—he must be a movie star." The chauffeur had opened the back door but I said to him, "Listen, I don't have to sit in the back seat. I want to sit up front with you. I don't need all this special treatment." He smiled and just said, "Whatever you like, Mr. Vergnes." I said, "Call me Jean." He smiled again.

We drove to the Beverly Hills Hotel, where I dropped off my luggage and changed into some fresh clothes. Ironically, as things turned out, I didn't spend a single night at the hotel the entire weekend, for the parties I went to lasted all night long. I remember returning to the hotel on Sunday, just before my flight, just so I could pick up my luggage. My first night in town, though, I was to go to Burgess Meredith's home, where a party was being held for all the people who would be on the show. There I had a chance to meet and talk with such celebrities as Burt Lancaster, Andy Williams, Carroll O'Connor, Gregory Peck, Larry Hagman, Robert Mondavi and, of course, Burgess himself. They were all so kind and most eager to share the French they knew with me. I would never have believed it if someone had told me while I was growing up that I would one day be in Hollywood, talking and discussing food with great film stars. But indeed I was, and it was quite enjoyable. I think we all sometimes forget just how down-to-earth celebrities can be. The party lasted until the early hours of the morning. It seemed that sleep was not a priority with these people. To keep up with them, I had to draw on my early experience as an apprentice, when I too would stay up all night long.

The next day we began taping the show. I had planned to prepare my Chicken Gismonda. As I was assembling the ingredients, Andy Williams, Carroll O'Connor and former senator Sam Ervin were behind me, chatting and cracking jokes. When I reached the wine I needed for the deglazing, I found Andy, Carroll and the senator sharing the bottle among themselves. They all had big grins on their faces. It was really a good time. After my demonstration, we were seated with Dinah, discussing things. At this point I remember Senator Ervin in particular, for whenever I said anything he would ask either Andy or Carroll what I had just said. At one point he said to me in his deep Southern accent, "Jean, I have a hard time understanding you—you have such a strange accent." I replied to the senator, "But sir, you have such a strange accent to me as well." We all had a good laugh over that.

It was certainly a memorable weekend. When I boarded the plane to leave I was exhausted. I asked the stewardess for a glass of soda, and when I arrived at Kennedy airport I awoke to find the glass still full from when I had first poured it. I had slept the whole way home.

Returning to Le Cirque, though, was by no means an anticlimax. I often remember the excitement and commotion generated whenever a celebrity walked in. If Richard Nixon came for lunch, the security guards were buzzing around the dining room, making sure everything was safe. If Imelda Marcos stopped in, the security and media would flock through the dining room as well. I couldn't think of a more appropriate name than "circus" when this kind of activity was going on. It was this kind of continuous excitement, I think, that made the celebrities return again and again. It was, and still is, a place for high-society people to be seen, and Sirio and I made sure they were catered to properly.

It is hard for me to explain what Le Cirque was, and still is, like. It is a place that must be experienced to fully appreciate what I find so difficult to convey. It is a unique combination of atmosphere, elegance and, of course, fine food. I also think that what made us so successful was that our foremost concern was always our clients. We were always showing our clients our concern for them by changing the chairs, silverware, plates and carpeting every year. A restauranteur must always keep putting money back into his establishment if he expects patrons to continue to dine there. If he forgets for one moment that the client is the number-one concern, then he will have sown the seeds of failure. I remember Sirio calling clients, or writing to them, if they hadn't been in to dine for a period of time. He would check to make sure that nothing had been wrong the last time they had come. It is this type of dedication to the client that makes a place successful. It is a testament to Sirio's dedication that today Le Cirque continues its tradition of excellence.

I derived an enormous amount of satisfaction from what Sirio and I accomplished during my years at Le Cirque, from 1974 to 1978. It came as quite a surprise to many people, as well as to my partner, when in late 1978 I decided to sell my share of the restaurant. Friends and family alike could not, and still do not even today, understand why I would want to leave so much so soon. The reason is that I had committed myself to certain opportunities that, for one reason or another, eventually fell through. But I have no regrets. I look into the past not to pose the question of "What if?" I look back to see the roots of my dream and to appreciate its culmination.

APPETIZERS

Cold Creamed Cyrano

2 cups sorrel
3 tablespoons butter
1 quart consommé (beef or chicken)
6 egg yolks
¼ pint heavy cream
Salt and freshly ground pepper to taste
Chervil leaves

1. Cut the sorrel julienne style, melt the butter, and then soak the sorrel in the butter until softened.

2. Add the consommé and sorrel to a soup pot and heat on moderate flame for 10 minutes. Remove from the flame and add the mixture of egg yolks and heavy cream to the consommé.

3. Put the soup back on the flame and allow to heat but not boil. Add salt and pepper and then refrigerate.

4. Before serving add some chervil leaves on top of the soup.

SERVES 6 TO 8

NOTE: Long, very thin slices of French bread that has been dried in the oven can also be added to the top of the soup. It is suggested that this soup be served on ice.

Cold Cream of Waterbury

1 quart consommé (beef or chicken)
2 tablespoons curry powder
6 egg yolks
¼ pint heavy cream
2 apples, peeled and chopped finely
   Salt and freshly ground pepper to taste

1. Add the consommé and the curry powder to a soup pot. Heat on a moderate flame for about 10 minutes, allowing the ingredients to reduce.

2. Mix the egg yolks and heavy cream together. Remove the pot from the flame and add the egg and cream mixture to the consommé. Blend thoroughly.

3. Place the pot back on the flame and allow to heat well without permitting it to boil.

4. Add the apples, salt and pepper to taste, and refrigerate.

SERVES 6 TO 8

NOTE: For best flavor, serve on ice.

Carpacio Toscane

2 egg yolks
1 tablespoon chopped parsley
4 anchovy filets, chopped
½ tablespoon chopped capers
5 cornichons (imported French gherkins), chopped
1 tablespoon chopped onions
½ tablespoon imported French mustard
  Juice of ½ lemon
  Salt and freshly ground pepper to taste
  Worcestershire and Tabasco sauces
1 lb. top butt or tenderloin of beef, very lean,
  sliced very thin like prosciutto

1. Mix the egg yolks, parsley, anchovies, capers, cornichons, onions, mustard, lemon juice, salt and pepper in a salad bowl.

2. Slowly pour the olive oil into the above mixture. Add a dash of Tabasco and Worcestershire sauces and mix thoroughly. Serve cold with the meat.

SERVES 6

Vegetable Terrine

½ lb. tender young string beans
1 lb. leaf spinach
2 large Idaho potatoes, sliced with skins
3 medium turnips
4 carrots
1 lb. fresh mushrooms, sliced
1 tablespoon each fresh basil, parsley, chives
1 tablespoon white wine
2 eggs
3 egg yolks
1 cup heavy cream
  Salt and freshly ground pepper to taste
1 tablespoon sweet butter

1. Butter a 2-quart loaf pan. Set aside in the refrigerator.

2. Blanch the string beans, spinach, and potatoes. Chop spinach after blanching and chilling to keep color.

3. Cook the turnips and carrots and pureé together.

4. Sauté mushrooms in butter and add basil, parsley, and chives. Add wine and reduce until dry.

5. Beat together the eggs, egg yolks, heavy cream, salt, pepper, and butter in a separate bowl.

6. Layer the loaf pan, working with the soft vegetables first. Pour a quarter of the egg mixture in the mold and then distribute the spinach evenly. Add the carrot-turnip purée. Lay string beans lengthwise in the mold; pour in another quarter of the egg mixture. In a separate bowl gently mix together the potato slices and mushrooms with remaining egg mixture. Pour into mold. Butter a thin-bladed knife and run gently around the edges of the molds to allow the custard to saturate the layers evenly. Cover with buttered aluminum foil (shiny side in).

7. Place the mold in a roasting pan and pour boiling water halfway up the side. Bake in a preheated oven, at 350° F, for 1 hour. Add boiling water if necessary during the baking period. To test for doneness, run a skewer into the center and remove—it should be dry.

SERVES 4

NOTE: Serve with Herbed Sauce (see page 225).

Curried Chicken Salad

2 cups diced cooked chicken
1 apple, peeled and diced
1 cup diced fresh pineapple
¼ cup golden raisins
⅓ cup chopped dates
2 tablespoons chopped chutney (including syrup)
½ cup shredded coconut
1 tablespoon curry powder
2 tablespoons chicken consommé
1 cup mayonnaise
½ teaspoon salt

1. Combine the chicken, apple, pineapple, raisins, dates, chutney, and coconut in a bowl. Sprinkle with salt.

2. Simmer curry powder in consommé for 2 minutes, stirring to a smooth paste. Cool. Add this paste to mayonnaise.

3. Stir mayonnaise and curry powder mixture into chicken mixture. Chill.

SERVES 4

Spinach Salad

½ *teaspoon Dijon mustard*
2 *teaspoons vinegar*
2 *tablespoons oil*
  Salt and freshly ground pepper to taste
2 *handfuls raw spinach leaves*
4 *medium-size fresh mushrooms, sliced*
4 *slices bacon, cooked to a crisp and chopped*
1 *teaspoon chopped onion*

1. Mix the mustard, vinegar, oil, salt and pepper in the salad bowl.

2. Add the rest of the ingredients, toss, and serve cold.

SERVES 2

Chef's Salad

⅔ *lb. lettuce: 2 parts iceberg, 1 part escarole, 1 part romaine*
2 *slices tongue*
2 *slices turkey*
2 *slices ham*
2 *slices Swiss cheese*
½ *tomato*
2 *hard-boiled eggs*
2 *green olives*
½ *cup French dressing (see page 71)*

1. Cut the lettuce, clean and rinse. Distribute the mixed salad combination amongst the two bowls.

2. Cut the meats and cheese julienne style and place on top of the lettuce.

3. Cut the eggs and tomatoes in quarters and decorate around the salad bowl. Place the olives on top and serve.

SERVES 2

PASTAS

Le Cirque's Spaghetti Primavera

1 bunch broccoli
2 small zucchini
4 asparagus spears, each about 5 ins. long
1½ cups green beans, trimmed and cut into 1-in.
    lengths
    Salt and freshly ground pepper to taste
½ cup fresh or frozen green peas
¾ cup fresh or frozen pea pods, optional
1 tablespoon peanut, vegetable or corn oil
2 cups thinly sliced mushrooms
1 teaspoon finely chopped hot, fresh, red or green
    chilies or about ½ teaspoon dried red pepper
    flakes
¼ cup finely chopped parsley
6 tablespoons olive oil
1 teaspoon finely chopped garlic
3 cups red, ripe tomatoes cut into 1-in. cubes
6 fresh basil leaves, chopped, about ¼ cup, or about
    1 teaspoon dried basil
1 pound spaghetti or spaghettini
4 tablespoons butter
2 tablespoons fresh or canned chicken broth
½ cup heavy cream, approximately
⅔ cup grated Parmesan cheese
⅓ cup toasted pine nuts

1. Trim the broccoli and break it into bite-size flowerettes. Set aside.

2. Trim off and discard the ends of the zucchini. Do not peel the zucchini. Cut the zucchini into quarters. Cut each quarter into 1-in. or slightly longer lengths. There should be about 1½ cups, no more. Set aside.

3. Cut each asparagus spear into thirds. Set aside.

4. Cook each of the green vegetables separately in boiling salted water to cover. The essential thing is to cook each so that it remains crisp but tender. The broccoli, zucchini, green beans and asparagus should take about 5 minutes. Drain well, then run under cold water to chill, and drain again thoroughly. Combine the cooked vegetables in a mixing bowl.

5. Then cook the peas and pea pods; about 1 minute if fresh, or 30 seconds if frozen. Drain, chill with cold water and drain again. Combine with rest of vegetables in the mixing bowl.

6. Heat the peanut oil in a skillet and add the mushrooms. Add salt and pepper to taste, shaking the skillet and stirring. Cook about 2 minutes. Add the mushrooms to the vegetables. Add the chopped chilies and parsley.

7. Heat 3 tablespoons of olive oil in a saucepan and add half the garlic, tomatoes, salt and pepper to taste. Cook about 4 minutes, stirring gently so as not to break up the tomatoes any more than necessary. Add the basil, stir and set aside.

8. Add the remaining 3 tablespoons of olive oil to a large skillet, also the remaining garlic and the vegetable mixture. Cook, stirring gently, just long enough to heat through.

9. Drop the spaghetti into boiling salted water. Cook until almost but not quite tender. That is to say, al dente. The spaghetti, when ready, must retain just a slight resilience in the center. Drain well. Return the spaghetti to the kettle.

10. Select a utensil large enough to hold the drained spaghetti and all the vegetables. To this, add the butter. When it melts, add the chicken broth, half a cup of cream and cheese, stirring constantly. Cook gently on and off the heat until smooth. Add the spaghetti and toss quickly to blend. Add half the vegetables and pour in the liquid from the tomatoes, tossing and stirring over very low heat.

11. Add the remaining vegetables and if the sauce seems too dry, add about ¼ cup more cream. The sauce should not be soupy. Add the pine nuts and give the mixture one fine tossing.

12. Serve equal portions of the spaghetti mixture in four to eight hot soup or spaghetti bowls. Spoon equal amounts of the tomatoes over each serving. Serve immediately.

SERVES 4 TO 8

Spaghetti with Fresh Goat Cheese

1 lb. spaghetti
2 tablespoons olive oil
½ teaspoon garlic
1 teaspoon chopped pine nuts
2 whole tomatoes, peeled, seeded, and diced
2 tablespoons chopped basil
4 oz. goat cheese
2 tablespoons butter
    Salt and freshly ground pepper to taste

1. Cook the spaghetti al dente.

2. Heat the olive oil in a skillet until very hot. Add the garlic, pine nuts, and sauté for a few seconds only.

3. Add the tomatoes to the garlic and pine nuts and simmer for 1 minute. Add the goat cheese and butter and mix well. Add salt and freshly ground pepper to taste.

4. Mix the sauce with the pasta, and serve it with the basil on top.

SERVES 6

Fettuccine Prosciutto

1 lb. fettuccine
1 egg yolk
1 cup heavy cream
¼ cup sweet butter
½ cup Parmesan cheese
4 oz. prosciutto, sliced
Freshly ground black pepper to taste

1. Cook fettuccine to your taste in rapidly boiling water with some salt.

2. While noodles are cooking, beat egg yolk lightly with fork and add cream.

3. Place drained noodles in hot serving bowl. Add butter, cheese, prosciutto. Toss noodles with fork and spoon until well blended.

4. Pour over cream mixture. Toss a little bit more. Add pepper to taste. Serve immediately.

SERVES 4

ENTRÉES

Côtes de Veau Belles des Bois
VEAL CHOPS WITH MORELS

⅓ lb. dried morels
6 veal chops, ½ lb.
   Salt and freshly ground pepper to taste
14 tablespoons butter
2 tablespoons finely chopped shallots
   Juice of half a lemon
6 tablespoons dry white wine
1 cup heavy cream
1 tablespoon madeira or dry sherry
¼ cup flour
1 cup chicken broth

1. Place the morels in a mixing bowl and add hot (not boiling) water to cover. Let stand until cool. Drain well and pat dry.

2. Sprinkle chops with salt and pepper; set aside.

3. Heat 4 tablespoons of the butter in a skillet and add the shallots. Cook briefly, stirring, and add the morels. Cook, shaking the skillet, about 3 minutes and add the lemon juice. Cover and cook about 5 minutes. Add 2 tablespoons white wine and cover. Simmer 5 minutes. Add the cream and cover and cook over relatively high heat about 15 minutes. At this point the cream should be fairly well reduced and thickened. Add salt and pepper to taste and the madeira wine. Swirl 2 tablespoons of butter into the sauce.

4. Dredge the chops in flour. Heat remaining 8 tablespoons of butter in a large skillet and add the chops. Cook over high heat about 5 minutes or until nicely browned on one side. Turn and cook about 15 minutes on the other side. Do no overcook or the chops will dry out.

5. Remove the chops to a warm serving platter. Pour off most of the fat. Add remaining 4 tablespoons white wine and cook briefly. Add the chicken broth and cook over relatively high heat until reduced to about ¼ cup. Return the chops to the skillet. Spoon and scrape the mushrooms over all. Stir. Serve the chops with the mushrooms in sauce spooned over.

SERVES 6

Escalope de Veau Vieille France

3 slices milk-fed veal (approx. 3 oz. each)
1 tablespoon flour
Salt and pepper to taste
1 tablespoon butter
9 mushroom slices
1 teaspoon champagne or cognac
⅓ cup heavy cream
1 teaspoon chopped black truffles (optional)
Fresh lemon

1. Dip the veal in flour, and then salt and pepper to taste.

2. Sauté the veal in butter two minutes on each side. Remove the veal from the pan. Sauté sliced mushrooms for 1 minute.

3. Add fine champagne or cognac and flambé. Then add heavy cream and truffles. Cook, and allow to reduce by half.

4. Squeeze a few drops of fresh lemon, and correct the seasoning. Serve with piping hot buttered noodles.

SERVES 1

Grenadin de Veau aux Raisins
TENDERLOIN OF VEAL WITH RAISINS

4 8-oz., ½-in.-thick slices of veal, cut from the leg
Flour for dredging
Salt and freshly ground pepper to taste
1 oz. bourbon
1 cup Brown Sauce (see page 66)
½ cup black raisins, already presoaked in water for a
    half hour
⅓ cup sour cream
4 cherry tomatoes, skinless
1 cup heavy cream
4 carved mushrooms, sautéed
2 cups fresh spinach purée
1 large diced pear

1. Dip the veal in flour, salt, and pepper.

2. Sauté veal 3 minutes on each side, and flambé with half of the bourbon.

3. Remove the veal from the pan. Add Brown Sauce and reduce by two-thirds.

4. Add raisins, sour cream, heavy cream, cherry tomatoes and remaining bourbon. Allow to cook for 1 to 2 minutes on medium flame and then pour sauce over veal.

5. Serve with the spinach purée, mixed with the diced pear. Decorate with the carved mushrooms.

SERVES 4

Trout Meunière with Pecans

4 10-oz. trout (see note)
¼ cup milk
　Salt and freshly ground pepper to taste
½ cup flour
¼ cup peanut, vegetable, or corn oil
½ cup pecan halves
　Juice of one lemon
2 tablespoons finely chopped parsley

1. Using a pair of kitchen shears, cut off the fins from the back and sides of the trout. Leave the head and tail intact.

2. Place the trout in a large pan and add milk, salt and pepper. Turn the trout in the mixture.

3. Remove the trout without patting dry and dredge on all sides in flour seasoned with salt and pepper.

4. Heat the oil and one tablespoon of the butter in a large heavy skillet and add the trout, lining them up neatly in the pan. Cook about 8 minutes or until golden and cooked on one side. Turn and cook 8 minutes longer. Baste often. The basting is important to keep the trout juicy.

5. Remove the trout to a warm platter. Sprinkle with salt and pepper.

6. Pour off the fat from the pan and wipe out the skillet. Add the remaining 4 tablespoons of butter and when melted, add the pecans. Cook, shaking the pan and stirring, until the butter becomes the color of hazelnuts. Do not burn. Add the lemon juice and pour the sauce over the fish. Serve sprinkled with chopped parsley.

SERVES 4

NOTE: The 10 oz. weight listed here is arbitrary. Larger or smaller trout may be cooked in the same manner, but adjust the cooking time accordingly.

Marinated Shrimp with Avocado

3 lbs. raw medium shrimp, in the shell
1 carrot, scraped and cut into several pieces
2 celery stalks, diced
1 bay leaf
1 small dried hot pepper
10 peppercorns, crushed
    Salt and freshly ground pepper to taste
½ cup very thinly sliced onion
2 cups salad oil
1 cup red wine vinegar
2 cloves garlic, finely minced
3 medium size tomatoes, peeled, seeded, and chopped
1 sweet red pepper, diced
½ cup chopped parsley
2 ripe avocados, peeled and cubed

1. Fill a saucepan, with enough water to cover the shrimp. Add the carrot, celery, bay leaf, hot red pepper, peppercorns, and salt. Bring this to a boil and simmer for 10 minutes.

2. Add the shrimp and cook for 2 minutes after it comes to a second boil. Allow the shrimp to cool in the broth.

3. Drain the shrimp, peel and devein them. In a large bowl, combine the onions, oil, vinegar, garlic, tomatoes, sweet red pepper, and desired amounts of salt and pepper. Stir in shrimp and chill for 12 hours.

4. Just before serving, add a goodly amount of fresh black pepper, the parsley, and the cubed avocado.

SERVES 8

Seviche Miro Florés

PERUVIAN STYLE

2 lbs. red snapper filets, in ½-in. dice
Juice of 4 lemons
Juice of 2 limes
1 medium-size onion, sliced very thin
¼ cup pitted green olives, sliced
1 teaspoon chopped coriander
1 chili pepper, finely chopped
4 tablespoons white vinegar
2 tablespoons vegetable oil
1 tablespoon chopped parsley
1 teaspoon Worcestershire sauce
Tabasco to taste
Salt and freshly ground pepper to taste
4 avocados, halved

1. Marinate red snapper with the lemon and lime juice for a period of 6 to 8 hours.

2. Strain the lemon-lime juice and place the red snapper in a large salad bowl. Add all of the remaining ingredients. Mix thoroughly, adding salt, pepper, and Tabasco to taste. Refrigerate overnight.

3. Serve in half an avocado.

SERVES 8

NOTE: This recipe can be prepared with scallops instead of red snapper.

Filets of Sole Marguery

1 tablespoon butter
1 tablespoon chopped shallots
4 large mushrooms, sliced
4 filets of sole
  Salt and white pepper to taste
¼ cup dry white wine
¾ cup Fish Broth (see page 68)
8 shrimps, cooked, peeled, and deveined
12 large mussels, scrubbed and debearded (cook and
    remove from shells)
1½ cups Fish Velouté (see page 69)
  2 tablespoons Hollandaise Sauce (see page 32)
  Chopped parsley

1. Place the shallots and mushrooms in a large buttered skillet. Top them with the sole filets. Sprinkle with salt and pepper, and add wine and fish broth. Cover with buttered wax paper the size of the skillet.

2. Bring the wine mixture to a boil and poach the filets very gently until cooked.

3. Remove the filets and mushrooms to a serving dish. Add to this the shrimp and mussels, and keep aside, warm.

4. Bring the wine mixture and 1½ cups of the fish velouté to a simmer for 2 minutes, stirring with a wire whisk. Add 2 tablespoons of Hollandaise Sauce. Pour the sauce on top of the filets of sole and glaze under broiler until golden brown. Sprinkle with parsley.

SERVES 4

Broiled Flounder

Salt to taste
4 large filets flounder
4 tablespoons vegetable oil
3½ cups white bread crumbs
8 teaspoons melted butter
Lemon, sliced
Chopped parsley

1. Salt the flounder, then dip in the oil and cover with the bread crumbs.

2. Baste in butter and broil on both sides until golden brown. Serve with lemon and parsley on top. Serve with Mustard Sauce (see page 34).

SERVES 4

Cassoulet

1 lb. navy beans
3 chopped onions
6 cloves garlic
1 lb. salt pork
1 lb. pork knuckle
1 small piece bacon rind
6 oz. salami
2 cloves
1 carrot
2 bouquets garni (thyme, parsley, and bay leaf tied
    in cheesecloth)
1 4- to 5-lb. duck or goose (oven ready)
6 tomatoes, chopped
1 tablespoon tomato paste
1 lb. fresh pork shoulder
1 lb. garlic sausage
4 country pork sausages
    Breadcrumbs
    Salt and freshly ground pepper to taste

1. Soak the beans for 8 to 10 hours the day before. In a heavy enameled casserole dish cook the following in salted water for 2½ to 3 hours: 1 onion, 2 cloves garlic, salt pork, knuckle of pork, bacon rind, salami, carrots, 2 cloves, and 1 bouquet garni.

2. In a stew pot prepare a stew with the goose or duck, tomatoes, tomato paste, 2 onions, 2 cloves garlic, 1 bouquet garni, and salt and pepper to taste. Cook the stew for 45 minutes to 1 hour. It should not be too runny.

3. Prepare another stew with the shoulder of pork and adding all the same ingredients as for the goose or duck stew.

4. Cook the garlic sausage in some of the liquid from the beans, and sauté the country sausage until well done.

5. Drain the beans and mix them with sauce from both stews. Salt and pepper to taste.

6. Rub a large earthenware dish with a clove of garlic and then cover the bottom of the dish with a bed of beans. Lay the goose stew, the pork stew, garlic sausages, and country sausages on top, and then cover the top with the rest of the beans. Cook this over a medium flame for a half hour.

7. Pour fat from the country sausages and stews over the bread-crumbs and then sprinkle on the beans. Put in the oven just to brown the breadcrumbs.

SERVES 8 TO 10

Poulet Sauté au Vinaigre
CHICKEN SAUTÉ WITH VINEGAR

1 2½-lb. broiler chicken (separated: 2 breasts, 2 legs)
3 tablespoons butter
  Salt and freshly ground pepper to taste
2 teaspoons shallots, finely chopped
1 clove garlic, finely chopped
2 tablespoons red wine vinegar
3 tablespoons dry white wine
½ cup Brown Sauce (see page 66)
1 cup diced fresh tomatoes
½ bay leaf
  Chopped parsley

1. In a saucepan, sauté chicken in 2 tablespoons of butter. Season with salt and pepper and sauté until brown on both sides and cooked through. Keep on the side, hot.

2. Drain the fat from the pan.

3. Add chopped shallots and garlic. Simmer for 1 minute. Add vinegar and white wine, and simmer until liquid is reduced by half. Add Brown Sauce, chopped tomatoes, bay leaf, and parsley. Let simmer for a few minutes. Remove bay leaf. Add 1 tablespoon of butter. Stir and pour over the chicken.

SERVES 2

NOTE: Can be served with broiled tomatoes.

Chicken Diable

Salt and freshly ground pepper to taste
1 2½-lb. chicken, split in two.
1 tablespoon vegetable oil
2 tablespoons Dijon mustard
½ cup white bread crumbs
2 tablespoons melted butter
2 broiled tomato halves
1 small bunch watercress

1. Salt and pepper the two chicken halves according to taste; then cover skin with vegetable oil.

2. Broil chicken on both sides for approximately 15 minutes total.

3. Remove from broiler and cover the bird with a thin layer of mustard and sprinkle, liberally with the white bread crumbs.

4. Then spoon the melted butter over the prepared chicken halves and put back in oven. Allow to cook at 350°F until the bird turns to a golden brown.

5. Garnish with broiled tomato halves and sprigs of watercress and serve very hot with either Sauce Maison (see page 224) or Sauce Diable (see page 121).

SERVES 2

Chicken Pot Pie

1 2½-lb. chicken, poached in chicken broth (about
    2-½ cups)
1 tablespoon butter
1 tablespoon flour
2 cups chicken broth
½ cup heavy cream
1 oz. Sherry wine
    Chopped parsley
    Salt and freshly ground white pepper to taste
4 mushroom caps, cooked
4 baby carrots, cooked
4 small white onions, cooked
1 tablespoon peas, cooked
2 puff paste ovals, pre-baked (see page 221).

1. Skin poached chicken and separate legs and breasts.

2. Place cooked chicken in 2 oval crocks.

3. In a saucepan, mix butter, adding flour, thoroughly with a wire whisk for 2 minutes. Add 2 cups of chicken broth and let simmer slowly for 5 minutes. Add cream, Sherry, chopped parsley, salt, and pepper to taste.

4. Place chicken and sauce in 2 oval crocks. Garnish with vegetables and top with a cover of puff paste. Serve piping hot.

SERVES 2

Steak and Kidney Pot Pie

1 lb. lean sirloin steak, in 1½-in. cubes
1 lb. lean veal kidney, in 1½-in. cubes
3 tablespoons vegetable oil
1 clove garlic, finely chopped
½ tablespoon finely chopped shallots
    Salt and freshly ground pepper to taste
8 mushroom caps, sauteed
8 baby carrots, boiled
8 small white onions, boiled
2 tablespoons of cooked peas
2 oz. Sherry wine
1 teaspoon chopped parsley
4 puff paste ovals, pre-baked (see page 221)
1 bouquet garni (thyme, parsley, and a bayleaf tied
    in cheesecloth)
3 cups Brown Sauce (see page 66)

1. In a saucepan, sauté the beef and veal kidney on a high fire in the oil. When meat is brown on all sides add the garlic and shallots and simmer for 2 minutes. Salt and pepper to taste.

2. Remove the mixture to a platter, discard the fat. Replace the mixture in the same saucepan. Add the bouquet garni and the Brown Sauce and let that cook gently for about 45 minutes, until the meat is tender.

3. Discard the bouquet garni and place meat and sauce in 4 oval crocks. Garnish with the vegetables, add the Sherry and parsley. Top with a cover of puff pastry. Serve piping hot.

SERVES 4

Fast Puff Paste

1 lb. sweet butter, cold
1 lb. all purpose flour, plus ¾ cup for rolling
1 teaspoon salt
1 cup cold water

1. Dice the cold butter into small cubes. Arrange a well in the flour and place the butter and salt in the center.

2. Add the water and combine all ingredients rapidly into a mass. Do not knead the dough.

3. At this point the dough will appear very lumpy (the butter is still in pieces), but it should hold together. Flour the working table generously. Roll the dough into a ⅜-in.-thick rectangle.

4. Brush the flour from the surface and fold one end in to the center of the rectangle.

5. Fold the other end in. Both ends should meet in the center. Brush away excess flour.

6. Fold the dough in half.

7. You now have one "double turn," giving you 4 layers of dough. Make 2 more double turns for a total of 3 altogether. This is the equivalent of 4 or 5 single turns, and is enough for fast puff paste. Store in the refrigerator until needed, up to one week.

SAUCES

Sauce Americaine

LOBSTER SAUCE

1 1½-lb. live lobster
1 tablespoon vegetable oil
5 tablespoons butter
  Salt and freshly ground pepper to taste
1 small onion, finely chopped
1 tablespoon finely chopped shallots
2 tablespoons finely chopped carrots
2 tablespoons finely chopped celery
1 teaspoon crushed garlic
1 tablespoon finely chopped leeks
  Pinch of dried thyme
1 tablespoon chopped fresh tarragon, or ½ teaspoon
    dried tarragon
1 small bay leaf
3 tablespoons cognac
½ cup dry white wine
3 tablespoons tomato paste
2 cups Fish Broth (see page 68)
1 tablespoon flour
  Pinch of cayenne pepper

1. Cut the lobster in the middle where the body and tail meet. Break off the claws and crack them. Split the body in half and remove the tough sac near the eyes. Scrape the soft liver and coral from inside the body. Put them in a small cup and set aside. Cut body and tail into pieces.

2. In a deep casserole heat the oil and 1 tablespoon of butter. Add the lobster (except the liver and coral) and cook, stirring and mixing, about 5 minutes. Add salt and pepper.

3. Add the vegetables—onions, shallots, carrots, celery, garlic, leeks—thyme, tarragon, and bay leaf and cook, stirring, for 5 minutes. Add 2 tablespoons of cognac and flame it. When flame dies, add the dry white wine.

4. Stir in tomato paste, 2 cups of fish broth, and correct the seasoning. Cover and cook 10 minutes.

5. Remove the lobster claws and tails. Leave the body in the casserole and set aside to cool.

6. Pour the remaining mixture, body solids and all, into a china cap or strainer. Press with wooden pestle into a saucepan, extracting as much liquid as possible from the body and solids. There should be about 2 cups liquid. Discard the solids. Bring the sauce to a simmer.

7. Add 2 tablespoons of butter to the coral and liver. Add the flour and mix to blend. Remove from heat and stir in the coral mixture.

8. Strain the sauce through a very fine chinois. Return the sauce to a saucepan. Bring to a simmer, adding cayenne, and stir.

9. Crack the tail and claws when cold. Take the meat and cut in bite-size cubes. Add to the sauce.

10. Swirl in the remaining 2 tablespoons of butter into the sauce and add the remaining tablespoon of cognac. Bring to a simmer and serve.

YIELDS ABOUT 2½ CUPS

NOTE: If you wish a richer sauce, add ½ cup of already-simmered heavy cream. Sauce can be used for all poached fish, seafood, mousse of sole, scallops, shrimp, crabmeat, and fried fish.

Sauce Maison

2 tablespoons finely chopped shallots
1 cup white vinegar
1 quart brown stock
3 tablespoons dry English mustard
4 cups Sauce Diable (see page 121)
1 teaspoon lemon juice
1 tablespoon Worchestershire sauce
  Salt and freshly ground pepper to taste
1 cup heavy cream
  Tabasco to taste

1. Place shallots and vinegar in saucepan and reduce by one third.

2. When the reduction is completed, add the stock, mustard, Sauce Diable, lemon juice, Worcestershire, salt and pepper. Allow ingredients to simmer to 5 minutes.

3. Add the cream and Tabasco and simmer for 10 minutes, strain, and serve.

YIELDS 1 QUART

NOTE: This sauce can be used for broiled beef, veal, and chicken.

Sour Cream Dill Sauce with Mustard

1 egg
2 tablespoons Dijon mustard
  Freshly ground pepper to taste
1 tablespoon sugar (optional)
4 teaspoons lemon juice
1 small onion, finely chopped
2 tablespoons finely cut dill
1½ cups sour cream
  Dash of Tabasco

In a bowl, beat egg and mustard well. Add the remaining ingredients except the sour cream and Tabasco. When all is mixed blend in the sour cream and Tabasco. Stir until well blended then chill.

YIELDS 2 CUPS

NOTE: Serve this sauce with Gravlax (see page 99) or any smoked fish.

Horseradish Sauce for Smoked Fish

1 cup heavy cream
2 tablespoons fresh grated horseradish
Juice of ½ lemon
Salt and freshly ground black pepper to taste

Whip the heavy cream. Add horseradish, lemon juice, salt, and black pepper. Mix well. Serve sauce on the side of the plate.

SERVES 4

NOTE: Serve with such fish as trout, smoked salmon and sturgeon.

Herbed Sauce

½ cup chopped greens (spinach, chives, basil,
*   parsley—a little fresh mint optional)*
2 egg yolks
2 tablespoons imported Dijon mustard
½ teaspoon salt
½ teaspoon white pepper
1 cup extra virgin olive oil
1 tablespoon red wine vinegar
½ teaspoon Worcestershire sauce
*   Dash of Tabasco*
*   Juice of ½ lemon*

1. Chop the greens and wring out the moisture through a cloth.

2. Beat the eggs, mustard, salt, and pepper, and add the oil slowly. Then beat in vinegar, Worcestershire, Tabasco, and lemon juice. Fold in greens.

DESSERTS

Soufflé Base

4 oz. sweet butter
4 oz. flour
1 oz. cornstarch
4 oz. sugar
½ quart milk
8 egg yolks
8 egg whites

1. Mix butter, flour, cornstarch, and sugar until well blended. Boil milk in a heavy saucepan. Add flour mixture to the milk. Stir until thoroughly mixed, then keep on a medium flame until the mixture becomes dry and does not stick to the pan.

2. Take the mixture off the fire and add the egg yolk slowly. Mix for at least 1 minute. Cool. Beat the egg whites stiff with 1 oz. of sugar and fold gently into the mix.

3. Butter four individual souffle cups of one six-cup soufflé mold and sprinkle with sugar. Fill the mold and cook at 375° F. for 25 to 30 minutes.

SERVES 4

Soufflé Parfume

VANILLA SOUFFLÉ:
Add 1 teaspoon vanilla extract to the mixture at step 2.

GRAND MARNIER SOUFFLÉ:
Add 1 oz. Grand marnier liquor to the mixture at step 2.

RASBERRY SOUFFLÉ:
Add ½ cup fresh rasberries at step 2. Roll in flour. Add to the mixture with ½ oz. rasberry liquor, and 1 teaspoon flavoring color or rasberry extract.

CHOCOLAT SOUFFLÉ:
Add ½ cup cocoa powder and ½ oz. of rum to mixture at step 2. Serve soufflé with whipped cream.

Vanilla Sauce with Grand Marnier

1 egg white
4 oz. sugar
½ quart milk
5 egg yolks
1 teaspoon vanilla extract
1 oz. Grand Marnier

Blend eggs, egg white and sugar completely. Boil milk. Then, add egg mixture to boiling milk, mixing continually with a wooden spatula. Allow to come to a boil and then take off the fire. Continue to mix for a few minutes. Add vanilla and Grand Marnier.

YIELDS ABOUT 2 CUPS

Kiwi Pie

CRUST:

> *8 oz. flour*
> *4 oz. butter*
> *½ cup water*
>   *Pinch of salt*

CUSTARD:

> *1 whole egg*
> *3 egg yolks*
> *½ cup sour cream*
> *1 cup heavy cream*
> *½ cup sugar*

> *12 kiwi fruits, peeled and sliced ¾ in. thick*
> *½ cup apricot preserves*

1. Blend the crust ingredients and spread into a 10-in. pie plate. Garnish with the sliced kiwi.

2. Blend the custard ingredients and top pie crust with the mixture. Bake for 25 minutes at 375° F.

3. When cold, glaze pie with the warm apricot coating. Refrigerate the pie for 20 minutes and serve.

SERVES 10

Baba Au Rhum

> 1 lb. bread flour
> ½ oz. salt
> 1¼ oz. sugar
> ¾ oz. yeast
> 6 eggs
> 6 oz. butter, unsalted and melted

1. Mix the flour, salt, and sugar together in a bowl until well blended. Dissolve the yeast in ½ cup of lukewarm water. Add dissolved yeast and 3 eggs to the dry ingredients. Work dough until smooth, with an elastic consistency. Add remaining 3 eggs, 1 at a time, mixing well after each egg until dough returns to an elastic consistency.

2. Slowly add the melted butter to the dough and beat it until it is well blended and smooth. Cover the dough with a damp cloth and place in a warm place until it doubles in size.

3. When dough has risen, punch down completely. Fill lightly 2 greased savarin molds about ⅓ full and let dough rise until it reaches top of molds. Bake in oven preheated to 400° F. for 35 to 45 minutes.

4. Remove Baba from molds while still warm.

SYRUP:

> 1 qt. water
> 1½ lbs. sugar
> Lemon, halved
> Orange, halved
> 1 teaspoon vanilla extract
> ½ cup rum

1. Bring water, sugar, lemons, and orange halves to a boil and simmer for about 3 minutes. After 3 minutes, remove lemons and oranges and add the rum and vanilla.

2. Soak Baba in hot syrup until well soaked, then lift out carefully and drain well. Serve at room temperature.

SERVES 20

EPILOGUE

THE FUTURE OF CUISINE

As a chef who has dedicated more than fifty years to this trade I have seen many changes take place. I began my apprenticeship at a time when one still had to put coal into the stoves to get them working. Now, it's a simple turn of the valve and, presto, gas flames. As regards refrigeration, in my day we used ice to keep things cold, which forced us to buy fresh produce every day. With today's refrigeration systems, produce can last for weeks. In my time, as well, everything that needed to be chopped, rolled, diced or crushed was all done by hand. Today, using a food processor, all these things can be done with the simple push of a button. What these recent developments have given chefs is an enormous amount of time saved in preparation. Countless hours of chopping produce by hand, carrying coal and lugging pounds of ice have all been reduced to a matter of seconds. And I'm sure the technology will continue to improve because that is the nature of our society.

Regarding changes in cuisine, I have seen food preparation progress from strict adherence to the principles of the Escoffier school (of which I am a student) to something that pays at least partial homage to the nouvelle-cuisine movement of the 1970s and, now, the even lighter cuisine movement of the '80s. Through all this upheaval I have seen many positive steps taken toward improving the art of cooking. Without question, one of the most important changes that has occurred as a direct result of the popularity of these various schools is the conscientious effort to continue to make food lighter and healthier. After World War II, the French masters who trained me were already taking steps to make the sauces lighter than they had been prior to the war. Even then, we were being taught to eliminate the roux (the mixture of flour and butter) used to thicken sauce, because it was what the public wanted. With the introduction of *la cuisine minceur* by Michel Guerard in the 1970s, the epitome of light and health-conscientious cuisine was reached. Though I have an enormous amount of respect for Michel—indeed, he is a very good friend of mine—I do not think his is the type of cuisine I would want to reproduce. I still believe there will always be room in this world for a chef like myself who prefers the robust food—provincial food like calves liver, calves head, stews and cassoulet. That is not to say that nouvelle cuisine is not the way of the future, because it is. French food and all cuisines are headed in that direction. Food will certainly be lighter, more delicate and more refined, with an emphasis on health and nutrition and a you-can-eat-it-with-your-eyes appeal.

I don't think it will be too long before we will come around to Michel's view. But what all young chefs starting out must remember is that Michel's innovative approach is founded on a thorough knowledge of classic French cuisine. He has been able to express his individual talent because he is working from a learned tradition. The great chefs of today—people such as Pierre Franey, André Soltner, Jaques Pépin, Raymond Vaudard, Paul Bocuse, Roger Vergé and Jean Jacques Rachou—are able to express their individual talents because they have all first learned the tradition that came before them. Each has learned the basic functions of the kitchen; all have apprenticed and become proficient at each station of the kitchen. A chef can certainly be good without knowing the requirements of each station, but if he or she wants a name that rings as familiar as those above, he or she will have to understand each position and be able to perform the required tasks efficiently.

In this country today—in California especially—we are seeing a revolution taking place that is much the same kind of gastronomic revolution that occurred in France hundreds of years ago. Much creativity is being displayed by American chefs, but it seems to me that a sense of identity is missing from their food. Many types of cuisine are confronting each other. One can see Mexican, Chinese, French and Italian influences all competing, often in the same dish. American chefs must learn that to build a roof the foundation must first be laid. When eating one of these dishes I have often made the analogy to contemporary art; I ask myself, what is it supposed to be?

Don't mistake me. I truly believe that in about twenty years America will have established its own legitimate culinary tradition. But first the smoke must clear. Much of the problem is that young American chefs often become skilled in only one regional style. Though it is good to work with the products of one's geographic area—indeed, in France we all first learned to work with the products of our province—a good chef must learn to work with all foods, whether they are intrinsic to his area or not. There must be a greater willingness on the part of American men and women to broaden their knowledge. It is not enough to complete a two-year apprenticeship at a culinary institution; each aspirant must assume the role of journey-man and work at every station of the kitchen to become proficient at each. Though my first love is sauces, I would never have become an executive chef at The Colony or a restaurateur if I had not first learned the station rotations and basics of cuisine. I always return to the basics, which is what makes French cuisine what it is.

My confreres will agree with me, I think, when I say that American cuisine will come into being only when it adopts the basics of cooking that were established by the French a long time ago. Once these basics are incorporated into a tradition that pays homage to all regional styles, once Americans write their own cookbook, then there will be American chefs who can justifiably be termed "innovative." But one must give credit where credit is due. This country has made great strides in the thirty-seven years I have been fortunate enough to live here. America has all the right ingredients for a great tradition. It has a wealth of diverse food products, a unique mixture of different peoples and the ambition to succeed. I think more and more young men and women—it is great to be able to mention women because in my time they were not accepted as members of the trade—realize there is money to be made in this field.

From a restaurateur's point of view I also feel the city-restaurant concept will continue to evolve. Although there will always be a few *grand luxe* restaurants turning profits, despite huge staffs and equally large overheads, I think this tradition is changing. I see restaurants becoming more casual, making it possible for them to attract a broader clientele. The restaurant of tomorrow will, I feel, have a seating capacity of seventy-five to eighty-five people. The menu will change every day, and many specials will be offered. But quality food for a good price will always be the key to attracting people. And I don't care what kind of restaurant one owns, if the proprietor does not know the business inside and out it will fail. The idea that four rich investors can buy a place and make it run on money alone is ridiculous.

As for restaurants outside of the city, I think the ideal approach will always be the *auberge*, or French inn, concept. I feel it is especially attractive to be able to drive out to such a place, where I can eat well, enjoy myself and relax for a couple of days. The ideal *auberge* is one that has twelve to fourteen rooms for sleeping, and a dining room of eight to ten tables, with lunch and dinner served six days a week. As I have said, food is, without question, a sustenance of life. But the idea that it can be so much more than that is what has given impetus to my search for culinary excellence.

INDEX

A

Aaron, Sam, 155
Ahrens, Thomas, 2
Aioli for Boiled or Steamed Vegetables & Fish (Garlic Mayonnaise), 179
à l'assiette serving, 188
Amato, Baron, 158
Americaine, Sauce, 222–23
Anchovies
  Carpacio Toscane, 200
Anglaise, Sauce, 150
Appetizers
  Billi-Bi, 160
  Bisque de Homard, 92–93
  Bouillabaise, 94–95
  Buckwheat Blinis, 105
  Caesar Salad, 140–41
  Canapé d'homard, 108–9
  Carpacio Toscane, 200
  Cheese Soufflé, 57
  Chef's Salad, 203
  Chicken Liver Pâté, 54
  Chilled Vichyssoise, 23

Clams with Blinis, 83, 104–5
Cold Creamed Cyrano, 198
Cold Cream of Waterbury, 199
Crêpes with Fine Herbes, 107
Croquettes of Crabmeat, 56
Cucumber Salad, 162–63
Curried Chicken Salad, 202
Delmonico Salad, 58
Fettucine Prosciutto, 206–7
Fish Chowder, 95–96
Foie Gras Salad, 102–3
Gazpacho, 162
Gravlax, 99–100
Guacamole, 163
Le Cirque's Spaghetti Primavera, 204–5
Les Endives Tombées, 24
Lobster Bisque, 92–93
Lobster Canapé, 108–9
Manhattan Clam Chowder, 136–37
Marinated Salmon, 99–100
Mousse de Sole au Vin Blanc, 97–98
Mousse de Truite, 98–99